# DON'T BE A SLAVE TO HOUSEWORK

# DON'T BE A SLAVE TO HOUSE WORK

PAM McCLELLAN

**BETTERWAY BOOKS**
CINCINNATI, OHIO

99  98  97  96  95      5  4  3  2  1

Library of Congress Cataloging in Publication Data

McClellan, Pam
    Don't be a slave to housework / by Pam McClellan.
        p.    cm.
    Includes index.
    ISBN 1-55870-356-X (pbk.)
    1. House cleaning. I. Title.
TX324.M35   1995
648'.5—dc20                                                    94-39467
                                                                  CIP

Interior design by Sandy Conopeotis-Kent

# ACKNOWLEDGMENTS

Thanks to all the homemakers who, over the years, have given me ideas, inspiration and fortitude to keep making things better.

Thanks to Bill Brohaugh at Betterway Books for his great ideas and excellent editing skills.

Thanks to Steve and Keegan who keep me on my toes and always on the lookout for an easier way.

To all the messies who want to be like me, this one's for you.

papers. Mess prevention and organizing tips room by room: Kitchen; Living room; Bathroom; Kids' rooms; Office.

The problem. The solution. Scenarios of housekeeping buga-boos and ideas on how to find solutions.

Doing your own thing; Your cleaners. Cleaning supplies. Other tools: Storing cleaners. Item cleaning vs. room clean-ing. First things first—have your plan. If it ain't broke, don't fix it. Bathrooms and kitchens: Cleaning the bathroom; Keeping up in the kitchen; Preventing the messes; Whistle while you work and clean up as you cook; A few odds and ends.

Quick cleanups: Things that can be done in two minutes or less; Five minutes or less; Ten minutes or less. Speedy Spiff-ups—quick answers to specific cleaning problems: In the kitchen; In the bathroom; Carpets; General. Company's coming: The living room; The bathroom; The kitchen; Emergency cleaning etiquette.

Garages; Kitchens; Laundry; Office. Buying new. Kitchens. Bathrooms. Around the house: Light fixtures; Floors; Furni-ture. Armed and dangerous.

# INTRODUCTION

Most of my friends and acquaintances know me as an organizer. "Pam's the one who has a place for everything. She's got a basket in her refrigerator for sandwich fixings. She knows exactly where to find a safety pin, the extra belt for the vacuum cleaner, the receipt for the television she bought last December, or a cancelled check from two years ago. She's got a storage system she uses for seasonal clothing, camera equipment and extra kitchen gadgets. She's even got a special box for wrapping paper and bows where she keeps extra tape and scissors. Something's wrong with her!"

Actually, something's right. Being organized is great. It's one of the things that keeps me from being a slave to housework. It's what makes housework tolerable and housecleaning possible.

If you think that I must be some sort of nut who spends all of her time disinfecting the plastic covers on the furniture, let me assure you, I'm not. It's precisely because I am not crazy about housework that I decided to master it. If *you* feel like a slave to housework, I understand. I used to do *everything* wrong. I had created so much unnecessary work for myself that though I was only in my twenties, I was burned out. I had no choice but to learn how to make things easier. It took me a while, but I made it. Now you can benefit from my experiences.

*Don't Be a Slave to Housework* is a companion to my first book, *The Organization Map*. That book showed you how to unclutter your home and organize it room by room and step by step. This book will show you how to lessen your housecleaning load by using time management skills, getting help from your family, uncluttering your home and decorating style, using conscientious cleaning methods and purchasing low maintenance furniture, carpets and appliances.

I know I must be doing something right because people have often asked me, "How do you do it? How do you keep your house so clean when you're so busy?" If you thought these words could never be applied to *you*, read on.

## Chapter One

# WANTED: HOMEMAKER. SUPERWOMAN NEED NOT APPLY

Would you answer an advertisement that read like this?

WANTED: Hardy woman to be available twenty-four hours a day, seven days a week for the next forty to fifty years. Successful applicant will demonstrate excellence in cooking, cleaning, shopping, washing, ironing, mending, folding, sorting, dusting, polishing, scrubbing, budgeting and decorating. Ability to bear children and get up several times a night to walk a crying baby a definite plus. Knowledge of basic first aid, how to fix a boo-boo, kiss an owie, make a tourniquet, and beat a fast path to the nearest emergency room essential.

Must know how to clean an oven, get a grape juice stain out of a beige carpet, and what to do about bubble gum in the baby's hair. Must be willing to taxi offspring to and from school, music lessons, friends' houses, band practice, sporting events, part-time jobs, the mall and so forth. Salary nonnegotiable—nonexistent. Fringe benefits include hugs and kisses and an occasional sleepless night.

A woman would have to be out of her mind to answer such an advertisement. Yet, how many of us actually wind up answering the call—homemaker, mother, housekeeper?

It seems that no matter how we slice it, housework and slavery go hand in hand. In fact, they seem to be made for each other. Just look at the way my *American Heritage* dictionary defines those words:

Housework: The tasks performed in housekeeping, as cleaning or cooking. (Rather a short definition for a job so long on work, I'd say.)

Slave: One bound in servitude to a person or household as an instrument of labor. A person who works extremely hard. (Your average mom.)

As I said, made for each other.

I suppose that every homemaker has felt like a slave to her home at one time or another. The endless cycle of doing and undoing, over and over, day after day, year after year. Like a hamster on a wheel, round and around she goes. . . . Ugh, I'm depressing myself.

Seriously though, anyone who has ever kept house knows what a challenge it is to avoid the incessant melee, planning, timing and proper execution of tasks are essential. In addition, there is your personal housekeeping philosophy—how important is housekeeping to *you*? What can you live with? What can you live without? How can you keep yourself going in circles without going crazy?

Before we get into the how's and have-to's of freedom from this slavery, let's look at my definition of housework.

*Pam's definition of housework:* Practically everything you do.

I'm being a bit whimsical, but sometimes it does seem that all we do is work.

Personally, I see housework as *any* work related to the function of hearth and home. In addition to the cooking and cleaning, there's the shopping, telephoning, paying of bills, weeding, checkbook balancing, and a million other "ings." I would include any and all chores, systems and routines employed in the perpetual cycle of housekeeping. I would even include taxiing the kids around to lessons, school and club meetings.

However, for our purposes we will narrow the definition. We will concentrate more on the routine cleaning and maintenance of the home. I'm not going to show you how to balance your checkbook or weed your garden. I will attempt to show you how I made cleaning easier for myself by changing the way I do things.

Unfortunately, most of us can't get away from housework. We can however, free ourselves from many of its *enslaving aspects*.

How do you keep from feeling like a slave to such a large and necessary part of your life? Well, first you must lay your foundation.

## YOUR FOUR CORNERSTONES

Any worthwhile construction project begins with a solid foundation. You are constructing a new way of life. In your effort to master housework, you need to build on the following four cornerstones. These are the core principles that will give shape and solidity to the cause for which you are working.

Mastering each of these principles will help you master housework. Not having control over even *one* can keep you a slave, physically or psychologically.

### 1. The Cornerstone of Organization

Being in control of the spaces, systems and routines in your home is essential to mastering housework. A lack of organization makes every task harder. You rewash the clothes you forgot about and left to mildew in the washing machine for three days. You make extra trips to the grocery store because you have no meal plan and forget ingredients. You're perpetually late for appointments because you can't find your car keys and your kids complain about wearing molding clothes to school. A lack of organization will have you running, shuffling and backtracking all day.

Being unorganized will keep you a slave to housework. This is a major cornerstone and you must master it if you are to free yourself. I wrote an entire book on this topic, *The Organization Map*. I'll give you some advice on the basics in chapter six.

### 2. The Cornerstone of Uncluttered Living

Nothing made me feel more like a slave than my own possessions. The very things I thought were precious were often those that kept me working round the clock.

Americans are drowning in clutter. It's all over the house, piling in the garage, spilling onto the patio and into the yard. I am convinced clutter has a detrimental effect on people. I think it weighs them down, wears them out, and keeps them from doing things they would do if not burdened by it. Unfortunately, most people don't have a clue as to how to identify and get rid of the stuff. They are so used to looking at clutter that they *overlook* it. I'll show you how to identify clutter and what to do with it in chapters six and seven.

### 3. The Cornerstone of Balance

If you are overwhelmed by demands on your time, attention and energy, it's easy for housekeeping to get short shrift. This leads to disarray, which leads to confusion, frustration and feelings of enslavement. Unless you can figure out how to increase the hours in a day (if you do, let me know) or how to speed up housecleaning à la Samantha in *Bewitched* (I'd like to be in on that too, please), then you will probably have to master the situation by getting rid of some of the housework, dropping some of your other obligations, or getting help with the housework. Getting help may mean enlisting previously unhelpful family members or hiring outside help. You'll get hints on help from the family in chapters four and five and outside help in the last chapter.

### 4. The Cornerstone of Realistic Expectations

If you feel that no matter how hard you work your house never seems clean enough, it could be that your expectations are unrealistic. Unrealistic expectations abound in our society and are very enslaving.

As a young homemaker I was anxious to run my home as well as Harriet Nelson (*Ozzie and Harriet*) and Betty Anderson (*Father Knows Best*) ran theirs. Those two TV supermoms were my idols as a child. They were the ultimate homemakers who made it all look so easy. They always looked lovely in their starched dresses, and handled every household crisis with grace and cheer. I wanted to grow up and run a home as smoothly and efficiently as they did. If they could do it, so could I. Of course, they weren't *actually* doing it, were they?

It's been many years since their faces graced the television screen and a lot of people now ridicule shows such as theirs as unrealistic. Perhaps they were unrealistic, but are the fads of our current popular culture any more realistic? I hardly think so!

These days you needn't settle for merely being an ideal homemaker. Not only can you have an immaculate house (apparently cleaning before 6:00 A.M.), you can also whisk off to your high-powered executive job, save the company from calamity, whisk back home to whip up a gourmet meal, help the kids with their homework (quality time), and then slip into your sexy lingerie for a passionate night with the hubby. If you survive, you can do it all again the next day. Honestly! Aren't you exhausted just *thinking* about it?

Where do all of these lofty expectations come from? Lots of places, but one source of unrealistic expectations is television and the media. Our *reality* is that we are surrounded by the *unrealistic*. Every day we are bombarded by ludicrous images. Have you ever wondered why that woman in the commercial for wrinkle cream is only twenty-one? Who has wrinkles at that age? And why is that woman scrubbing her tub in designer jeans? (I always wear silk myself. You just never know who might stop by.)

Advertisers using television to market products would have you believe that if you drink a particular brand of low calorie soft drink, you will have a figure like a supermodel. Or, if a man drinks a certain brand of beer, gorgeous women will come out of the woodwork to be with him. Much advertising seems to have the same theme: If only you would buy our product (you pitiful creature), your life would be transformed, and attractive members of the opposite sex will beat a path to your door. You know what? Some people actually fall for it! So what's my point?

## YOU JUST CAN'T HAVE IT ALL!

Did you hear me? I said, *You just can't have it all*. Of course, you want it all. Who doesn't? But you can't have it all.

Oh, I concede that there may be a few supermen and superwomen out there who can juggle a fabulous career, an active social life, and a perfectly clean house; raise brilliant, well-mannered children; romance their spouse; exercise daily; and write a novel, all while running for Congress. However, I've never met anyone like that. Not even one measly super person. It's simply not realistic. Something has got to give and some things have got to go. Superheroes are for comic books.

### Overcoming the Superwoman Syndrome

If Superman was less than perfect (remember kryptonite), why can't you allow yourself the same luxury? Besides, aren't you just sick and tired of other people setting ridiculous standards and then expecting you to kowtow to them? Of course you are.

If you are ready to step down from superdom, there are two things you need to do.

*First* of all, quit comparing yourself to everybody else. Many home-makers vastly overrate the housekeeping acumen of their friends and neighbors. Most aren't nearly as gifted as you imagine. Besides, to make an equitable comparison, you would have to compare things like how many kids of what ages are in the home, how much time is available for housekeeping, personal energy levels and even decorating styles. So stop comparing yourself to others!

*Second*, decide what you want out of life. This helps put housework into perspective. It's important, but it's not all-important. Somewhere along the line I decided there was more to *my* life than keeping a spotless home. There were things that I wanted to do, learn and accomplish. I didn't want to end up with an epitaph that read: "Here lies one heck of a housekeeper. Never did much else with her life, but she sure could mop a floor."

## THE WONDERFULLY NORMAL HOMEMAKER

Now that you've come back to your senses and your alternate person-ality — a normal homemaker — what can you expect?

Actually, that's up to you. Your preferences and needs will differ from everyone else's, and you need to determine what it is that *you* want.

Most likely, you can have more than you realize. Just by establish-ing your four cornerstones, you can maintain a fairly comfortable lifestyle with a reasonable amount of effort. The fussier you are (or the higher your standards) the more work will be required. It really comes down to what you are *willing* to *work* for. (You never actually can escape the *work* part.)

Deciding which housekeeping tasks are worthy of your best effort should help you get a clearer picture of your priorities.

### Exercise in Priorities

On a scale from one to five, one being very important and five being least important, rank these household tasks. Then, on the line next to them, jot down how often you think you need to do this task so that it will meet your personal standards.

D = Daily
T = Two or three times a week
W = weekly
Bi = Twice a month
M = Once a month
S = Seasonally

| TASK | IMPORTANCE | FREQUENCY |
|---|---|---|
| Prepare meals | _____ | _____ |
| Wash clothes | _____ | _____ |
| Iron | _____ | _____ |
| Mend | _____ | _____ |
| Do grocery shopping | _____ | _____ |
| Do household shopping | _____ | _____ |
| Scrub bathrooms | _____ | _____ |
| Pay bills | _____ | _____ |
| Clean mirrors | _____ | _____ |
| Polish furniture | _____ | _____ |
| Wash windows | _____ | _____ |
| Dust baseboards and frames | _____ | _____ |
| Make beds | _____ | _____ |
| Clean the kitchen | _____ | _____ |
| Mop floors | _____ | _____ |
| Dust | _____ | _____ |
| Vacuum carpets | _____ | _____ |

By ranking the tasks, you can ease some of the anxiety you get when wondering how you're going to keep up with everything. Not everything is of vital importance and not every task needs to be done daily. Once you establish which things are your main concerns, you can begin to set your goals. You can relax about the fives and make a plan for the ones. By the way, if you wound up with a bunch of ones, you are still clinging to that cape! If so, redo the list and rethink what you really feel is most important.

## Chapter Two

# DEVELOPING YOUR HOUSEKEEPING PLAN

## GOALS

When you're watching football, what is your favorite part of the game? Undoubtedly it's when your team scores a touchdown. It's exciting to see all their hours of hard work and practice culminate in reaching that goal.

Seeking to score more points than their opponent by reaching that goal line more frequently is why your team plays the game. Without that goal line to aim for, fight over and run toward, your favorite team could run all over the field for nothing. Running in circles, going out of bounds, fumbling the ball, what would it matter? They could get out there and jitterbug (I think they sometimes do) and it wouldn't bring them one step closer to winning the game. Without a goal, why would they even bother to play the game? Without a goal, there *is* no game.

## GAME PLANS

In addition to having a clear goal, football teams understand the need to have a game plan. A coach doesn't just point to the goal line and tell his players, "Get the ball and run that-a-way." Carefully contrived plays move your team down the field to their goal.

Without a goal to run toward and a plan to get them there, your favorite team will never score. If they don't score, they don't win. It's the same for you. You can run yourself ragged all day, but without a goal and a plan, you'll never score.

## ONE OF THOSE DAYS

Have you ever had "one of those days?" First, you oversleep because the alarm didn't go off. When you wake up, you realize you've got twenty minutes to get the kids up and out of the house. While you're in the kitchen trying to fix breakfast (it'll have to be dry cereal because you're out of milk), your teenage daughter starts screaming from the shower that you are out of shampoo. Your sleepy nine-year-old comes downstairs wearing two different shoes and his pajama shirt. You wonder if anyone will notice. The seven-year-old complains that she can't find any clean clothes to wear. You rush to her closet where you find two choices: the grass skirt you bought when vacationing in Hawaii and a pinafore that hasn't fit her since she was three. You decide to keep her home. She looks a bit flushed anyway.

The children miss their buses, and you have to drive them. While dropping your son off you spot the nine-year-old's teacher and tell the child to search for pennies and gum wrappers on the floor of the car. On the way home you stop for groceries. "At least *something* has gone right this morning!" you think to yourself. That is, until you realize you are out of checks. Your attempt at searching the bottom of your purse for $143.67 in spare change is futile.

The day continues in the same fashion and you contemplate hara-kiri over supper. At the end of the day, you fall into bed exhausted, wondering how you could have run so much and accomplished so little.

*Everyone* has had days like that. Many homemakers feel trapped because they have no plan to help them get their work done. They are busy, they are moving and working, but they zigzag their way through the day and have little to show for their effort.

In order to achieve your goal of mastering housework you need a *game plan*. That game plan is your housekeeping schedule.

## YOUR GAME PLAN—YOUR SCHEDULE

Before you start hyperventilating at the thought of having to use a schedule, give me a chance to explain. First, think about this. When do you usually do your laundry? How about the grocery shopping? If your answer was, "Whenever I feel like it," you have lots of company. The trouble is, seldom does one feel like scrubbing the bathroom or mopping the floors.

When I was feeling like a slave to housework and was willing to try anything to improve the situation, I decided it was time to try a schedule. I was apprehensive, but I did it anyway. That's when I discovered what a luxury it was. (Alright, convenience.) In fact, scheduling has made my life so much easier that I can't imagine going back to the haphazard way I used to do things.

In my quest for freedom, I came to understand an important distinction between the work I was doing and my feelings of enslavement. I found that my feelings of bondage were not always related to how *hard* I worked. Frequently they resulted from the *way* I approached doing the work. I had thought my method of cleaning when I got around to it was a way of being easy on myself. Instead, it made everything harder.

It's the same for you. You understand the frustration you experience when you stand dripping wet in the shower and discover you are out of shampoo. The humiliation you go through when you realize you are out of checks just as the cashier has totaled your grocery order. The aggravation of never having a clean outfit for work in the morning. All of these trials are related to not scheduling the work.

Using a schedule is not really an extraordinary idea. Millions of people do it every day. In business, some people refer to their schedule as their itinerary, agenda, appointment log or daily calendar. Whatever name you give it, it's the same concept — planning the day so you know what you will be doing and when you will be doing it.

If you don't take control of the way you do your housework, you'll end up doing it only when you are backed up against a wall. Surrendering control keeps you a slave. Scheduling helps put you in control. In the previous chapter, I said you can't have everything. However, if you want *anything*, you had better make it a goal and run toward it. Henry David Thoreau is quoted as saying, "Things do not change; we change." If you want to achieve your goals, you had better change. So, learn how to set and score goals.

## GOAL SETTING TIPS

*Pinpoint your goal.*

Be specific. For instance, "My goal is to always have clean clothes for work so that I won't run around at the last minute."

### Create a realistic game plan that will take you to your goal.

"I will achieve this goal by doing my laundry on Monday and Wednesday evenings. Monday evenings I will iron the outfits I have chosen for Tuesday and Wednesday. Wednesday evenings I will iron the outfits I have chosen for Thursday, Friday and Monday."

### Put it in your playbook (schedule).

Once you know your goal and have a game plan to get you there, put it in your permanent playbook. Schedule that play into your daily routine just like coaches schedule their practices.

### Make the decision to follow through.

Have you ever been determined about something and decided you were going to do it? Then what happened? You *did* it, didn't you? You have to *decide* to achieve your goal. If you are not willing to make this decision, you are not serious enough about your goal.

### Condition yourself with practice.

How does your favorite football team win games? They practice, practice and practice some more. If you examine your own accomplishments, you'll see that prior to the achievement came *practice*. Whether it be playing piano, learning to cook or mastering your backhand, it took practice to get to your goal. The same is true for housekeeping goals. You won't turn into "Susie Homemaker" overnight, but follow your schedule and with repetition you will become better at reaching your goals.

### Remember the point of the game.

When a football player fumbles, he can't turn to his teammates and say, "I blew it, I'm going home." Your life is far more important than any football game. If you fumble, get up and get back into the game. Remember to keep your eye on the goal and keep running toward it.

## More Good Reasons to Use a Schedule

1. It's tailor-made for *you*. You plan activities at your own convenience.

2. It lets you know when you will be doing a particular job and consequently, when you will *not* be doing others. It lets you off the

hook because there's no need to torture yourself about when you'll get a chance to do something.

3. You can schedule fun time. Your schedule doesn't just have to be for chores. Plan your fun activities as well and you have built-in motivation to get the work done.

4. You enjoy a genuine sense of completion when your work is through. If you have no beginning and end to your daily work, it seems as though you are never finished. Your schedule allows you to enjoy your off time.

5. After a while, your schedule becomes such a matter of routine that you forget you use one. I've been following a schedule for ten years now and no longer think about it. In fact, I don't even look at my schedule because it comes so naturally.

Your schedule should be seen as a help, not a hindrance. It's there for your benefit. If something more interesting comes along (your husband or a friend calls and asks to meet you for lunch), you can always indulge yourself and catch up the next day. Using a schedule on a regular basis affords you the opportunity to goof off once in a while without guilt. It's when we have no rhythm to our work that we can get overwhelmed.

## Setting up the Schedule

Now that I've convinced you of the benefits of using a schedule, let's look at exactly what should be placed on a schedule and how to set one up.

My main concern is for you to set a schedule for your weekly or twice-weekly routine tasks. I do not recommend that you list your daily chores. Things such as bed making, meal preparations and so forth are so commonplace that it is not necessary to list them. However, if you would prefer to list them, by all means do so.

Following is a list of typical weekly chores. Check off those you want to include in your schedule.

| | |
|---|---|
| ☐ laundry/ironing | ☐ grocery shopping |
| ☐ changing linens | ☐ mopping floors |
| ☐ cleaning mirrors | ☐ dusting/polishing furniture |
| ☐ vacuuming | ☐ cleaning out the fridge |
| ☐ cleaning the oven | ☐ watering plants |

☐ paying the bills          ☐ mending
☐ scrubbing the bathrooms   ☐ _____
☐ _____   ☐ _____

On the lines provided, jot down any other jobs you want to do. By the way, you may not do all of the things I listed. Perhaps you send your mending out. Maybe your spouse pays the bills. All the better for you. Just check off the items you want on your schedule.

## Blocking in Time on Your Schedule

Now that you have identified *what* it is you want to do, let's identify *when* you are available to do it.

You may find this easier to do if you approach it backward. Using the chart provided on page 16, mark off all blocks of time when you will be unavailable for cleaning tasks. If you work outside the home, block in your work schedule, the time it takes you to get ready in the morning and your travel time. Block in any other times when you are not available. For instance, when you pick your kids up from school, when you take your daughter to her piano lesson, or when you volunteer at the hospital.

Next, determine when you just plain don't want to be doing housework. In other words, if your weekends are sacred to you, plan to do only your daily chores then. If Wednesday has traditionally been your day out for fun shopping or lunch with your friends, plan to leave Wednesday free from housework. This backward process should automatically leave you with blocks of time that can be used for chores.

Next, determine how you want to get the work done. Perhaps you can schedule one long day of housecleaning per week. Or, if you would prefer, a little each day. You may find it helpful to look at the sample of my schedule on page 17. As you can see, I spread things out and don't overburden myself on any one day. On the other hand, it may work better for you to have one marathon cleaning day. I know one woman whose cleaning day is Tuesday. She cleans her house from top to bottom and never accepts any invitations for events falling on Tuesday. That's how she has done things for years and that's how she prefers it. That's the beauty of the schedule. It's tailor-made to your own specifications.

### Sorry, We're Closed

Years ago I knew a woman who ran a little business. She had high hopes for its success, yet she had a carefree attitude about it. For the first time in her life she was the boss and it felt good to be in charge.

Not having anyone to answer to made her think that she could run her business the way she wanted to. Why, if something came up, she could simply put up the "closed" sign and take off. The temptation to dart off to sales, run a few errands, and take off for one reason or another increased over time. Pretty soon she started getting behind. Paperwork wasn't getting done and she was often short on inventory. She even began losing her regular clientele.

She had thought that she was doing herself a favor by running her business in this carefree manner. She was able to come and go as she pleased. With no one to answer to, she was in and out at her own whim. In actuality, she had her *customers* to answer to. People became fed up with her irregular business hours. They never knew if the store would be open or not. She also had creditors and product representatives to answer to. With her unpredictable schedule, they had difficulty reaching her and she got a reputation for being unprofessional. Her business was in trouble.

Perhaps you think this is a crazy way of doing business. How could an intelligent person even consider acting in such a way? Well, the truth is that you are an intelligent person and chances are, if you do not use a schedule for housework you are running your home in much the same way as this woman ran her business. Whenever you take the attitude that you can "close up shop" and do your work when you find the time you are in a losing venture.

Also, your schedule may change periodically. Don't worry that once you've made a decision, you must stick to it for life. I have often rearranged my schedule as my needs changed.

| | MONDAY | TUESDAY | WEDNESDAY | THURSDAY | FRIDAY | SATURDAY | SUNDAY |
|---|---|---|---|---|---|---|---|
| **Morning** | | | | | | | |
| **Afternoon** | | | | | | | |
| **Evening** | | | | | | | |

| | MONDAY | TUESDAY | WEDNESDAY | THURSDAY | FRIDAY | SATURDAY | SUNDAY |
|---|---|---|---|---|---|---|---|
| **Morning** | MORNING DAILIES laundry scrub bath(s) mop floors dust + polish vacuum 10:30 A.M. | MORNING DAILIES office hours phone calls pay bills write letters | MORNING DAILIES clean refrigerator grocery shopping | MORNING DAILIES laundry scrub baths dust vacuum | MORNING DAILIES off the rest of the day | MORNING DAILIES | OFF! |
| **Afternoon** | *Afternoon time is available for work other than housework and/or other interests* | | | | | | |
| **Evening** | dinner | dinner | leftovers | dinner | FUN night | dinner | |
| | PM DAILIES (clean up after dinner) | PM DAILIES | PM DAILIES | PM DAILIES | PM DAILIES | PM DAILIES | |
| | Pick up | Pick up | Pick up | Pick up | Pick up | Pick up | |

## DESIGNATE * ELIMINATE * CONTAIN

When pressed for time, we sometimes wonder if certain things are worth doing. When determining how to fit a particular housekeeping task into your schedule, it may be helpful to put it through this three-step thought process.

### 1. Designate the worthiness of the work.

Determine how important this job is to you. Obviously, laundry will be a high-priority task. Polishing doorknobs *should* be low priority. (Don't laugh. Polished doorknobs are essential for some.) Making beds may fall somewhere in between. If you are in a particularly busy stage of your life, schedule only the high-priority tasks and allow yourself the luxury of not worrying about the others until your life is less hectic.

To further illustrate, if you are unsure of the importance or effect of a particular chore, determine its merit by answering the questions below.

- Does this job affect my daily life?
- What would happen if I didn't do this job every day?
- What would happen if I didn't do this job once a week?
- Is this a job I can delegate to someone else in the family?
- Is this a job I can pay someone else to do?

### 2. Eliminate all aspects of the work that are unnecessary or unimportant to you.

This is especially important for the household jobs that you find least tolerable. Dusting falls into my "least tolerable" category. Consequently, I have virtually nothing that needs dusting. I used to have loads of things, but I wised up.

When faced with a task you find distasteful, figure out what *aspects* of that task can be eliminated.

- Hate dusting? Do as I did and get rid of the dust catchers.
- Hate hand washing clothes? Get rid of such delicates and go back to easy wash and wear.
- Hate to cook? Double, triple or quadruple recipes and drastically reduce the time spent cooking.
- Hate to grocery shop? Have the store deliver.

**It Just Happened**

Several years ago I was conversing with a young woman who is a devout Christian. She related a story about some spirited debates she and her classmates had engaged in with a teacher. This group of students all shared the same religious convictions but the teacher did not. One day a student asked; "Well, if you don't believe in God, how do you explain the creation of the universe?" With a shrug the teacher answered, "It just happened."

The next time the class met, the teacher was surprised to see a three-dimensional model of the solar system on his desk. Looking at the class he asked, "Where did this come from?" The students all feigned innocence. Finally one said, "I guess it just . . . happened!"

In life, things don't just happen. Groceries don't magically appear in the refrigerator, clothes don't mysteriously wash and iron themselves, and bathrooms are not self-cleaning. (Rats.) If we want something to happen, we have to *make* it happen. So, make your schedule and *make* things happen.

- Hate to iron? Hire it out or find a friend you can trade off with. (You'll do her mending if she does your ironing, etc.)

Many chores can be made more palatable by eliminating unnecessary aspects.

### 3. Contain the amount of time spent on the work.

This is important chiefly for the sake of sanity. Any job, even a quick one, can be successfully dragged out over an entire day. (I was the champ at this.) This sort of avoidance usually works against you because not only does the job go undone, the guilt keeps you from having any fun. This is why I recommend putting a cap on the amount of time you will spend on a particular job. I don't suggest you time yourself down to the minute, but you needn't allow four hours to mop the kitchen floor, either.

Just putting a plan on paper to complete a particular job by a certain marker (before lunch, before the kids get home from school, etc.) can give you the little push you need to meet your own goal. I use the three natural segments of the day as my markers. My weekly chores are arranged so that I can easily complete them before lunch. I seldom have an afternoon job, but if I did I would set a goal to have it done before starting dinner. Likewise, if I take on an evening project, I work to complete it before 10:00. I find having a cap keeps me going so I can complete the work as quickly as possible.

By doing yourself the favor of charting a reasonable schedule for your routine housekeeping chores, you take the first step toward mastering housework by organizing your time.

## Chapter Three

# HELP FROM YOUR FAMILY

## RALLYING THE TROOPS

In your quest to master housework, you need allies. You have some (believe it or not) right under your nose: your own family members! Now, before you start complaining that your family does more to *increase* your slavery than to relieve it, give me a chance to explain.

First of all, I won't argue that children are a lot of work, especially when very young. But, as they grow, so does their ability to contribute. Even if you have never had any volunteers, you can still expect and get some cooperation from your kids. In this chapter I will share some tips on how to get them to pitch in with chores around the house.

As for that *other* member of the family, your beloved spouse, that may be a trickier matter. We'll delve into that in the next chapter.

## UNITED WE WORK

If you are concerned that assigning children housekeeping chores is an unfair burden to them, let me quell those fears. There are several good reasons to have children pitch in with housework. Here are a few:

1. To lessen *your* load. If you are less harried and stressed you will have more fun time with the family.

2. To teach them skills that they will need once on their own. I'll never forget a television interview I once saw with movie director Oliver Stone. He was relating a tale of a time while serving in Vietnam. Some of his buddies were kidding him because he didn't know how to operate a can opener. He explained that he had grown up

in a family that had employed maids. There was never any reason for him to open a can by himself. While his story may be an extreme, many young people leave for college without a clue about basic laundry, sewing, cooking or other housekeeping skills. On top of the pressure of higher education and being away from home, they have to figure out how to take care of themselves! Parents who do not prepare their children for adulthood do them no favor.

3. To teach them responsibility. Contributing in this way helps to impart an understanding that we all have obligations that must be met, fun or not.

4. To give them an opportunity to learn cooperative skills through teamwork. They will learn about sharing, compromising, and working together for a common cause.

5. To bolster self-esteem. Being able to effectively complete necessary tasks can give your children a sense of pride in themselves. They will know they are competent, capable people.

6. To help them respect *your* work. They will have a greater respect for the work that Mom does if they do some of it themselves.

Still, the question remains, how do you get them to help?

## GETTING THEM IN GEAR

You may have noticed that revving the engine makes a lot of noise, but it doesn't get you anywhere if you're still in "Park." Quit with all the noise (nagging) and get into gear so you can move forward. Here's what you can do:

### 1. Discuss your plans with your children.

If helping around the house is something your children are unaccustomed to, then you need to sit down with them and lay out your plans. Don't be afraid to tell them you need help. Explain that you will have more time for doing things with them if you get some help with housework. Tell them you intend to get the house organized and decluttered to reduce the work. Explain what you expect; for them to keep their own rooms tidy, to do one weekly chore, and to help with general daily pickup, for instance. If you think this is too much to expect all of a sudden, then ease them into whatever program you have in mind. Perhaps begin with the responsibility of keeping their own room clean. Eventually they can help with nightly kitchen cleanup and general daily pickup throughout the house. Lastly, they may take on a weekly chore.

## 2. Determine incentives.

Until they have matured enough to have their own internal motivation for getting something done, children can be persuaded to do things by receiving external rewards. If they know they can get A by doing B, you may have some very handy helpers around the house. Make a list of things (items, activities, privileges — even money) that your children enjoy and use them as incentives for your kids to get things done.

The only drawback to offering incentives is that you may start trying to outdo yourself, offering bigger and better privileges all the time. If this happens, the child is less likely to become internally motivated and will be more dependant on external rewards.

Perhaps you are of the opinion that children should have responsibilities without expecting rewards. I agree. However, it is true that giving a person a good *reason* for performing a task does encourage them to get up and do it.

If you are completely against giving rewards for routine work, you may consider a compromise. For instance, they don't get any money for keeping their rooms clean, but they do get money (or rewards) for weekly jobs. The incentive for keeping their room clean is a negative incentive; to avoid the punishment they will get if they don't. The incentive for cleaning the bathroom once a week is a positive incentive; the pocket money they need, or another fun thing. Positive incentives should be offered whenever possible. Incentives may be anything from a trip to the park, zoo, museum, a pool party or slumber party, a movie, toy, privilege such as use of the car, whatever. Ask them for ideas and jot them down.

## 3. Consider merits and demerits.

Similar to the idea of giving money or rewards for work is the idea of collecting merits. For instance, you may give a merit for various chores (some may be worth several merits) and when a particular total is met, the child can claim a reward. You may do this in levels. For instance, five merits may earn them an in-house privilege: an extra television program, bedtime one hour later this weekend, or more time playing video games. Ten merits may give them an outside reward. They can go to a movie, a concert, to a sleepover and so forth. This approach will also give them a chance to use decision-making and budgeting skills. They can use their five merits now, or save up until they have ten.

Demerits are incentives in reverse. If a task is not performed on time and mother has to do it, the child is given a demerit. When they understand the cost of not performing the task, they should straighten up.

### 4. Teach them how to clean.

Children aren't born with this knowledge. Before you expect them to pitch in, you'll have to invest some time in teaching them how to do each job, safety precautions to take and so forth. An eight-year-old will probably not do a job as well as a fifteen-year-old. If they have done the best they can do but it is still not up to your standards, relieve them of that chore and assign a more appropriate task.

### 5. Create chore charts for each area.

It would be beneficial to make up chore charts for each job or area of the home with which you want your family to help. For instance, if you are going to expect your fourteen-year-old to clean the bathroom once a week, you should have a chart posted that will indicate everything you expect to be done (see illustration on page 25). Chore charts are beneficial for everyone because they leave no room for guesswork. A helper knows exactly what needs to be done and can even check off each aspect of the job as it is completed. When you check the work, you have a reminder of what you requested.

Chore charts should be posted in an inconspicuous place in the area they pertain to. Use a Velcro pencil holder to keep a pencil handy in the same location. Indicate weekly shifts by dating the slots above the job description (as in illustration).

### 6. Offer compliments and praise.

Parents who ask their children for hugs and kisses know how wonderful it feels to have their request granted. About the only thing

**BATHROOM
CLEANING CHART**

| | | | | | | | | | | | | | |
|---|---|---|---|---|---|---|---|---|---|---|---|---|---|
| *Scrub sink and chrome* | | | | | | | | | | | | | |
| *Scrub tub and shower door* | | | | | | | | | | | | | |
| *Scrub toilet bowl* | | | | | | | | | | | | | |
| *under seat* | | | | | | | | | | | | | |
| *under lid* | | | | | | | | | | | | | |
| *base* | | | | | | | | | | | | | |
| *Wipe down counters and shelves* | | | | | | | | | | | | | |
| *Clean mirror* | | | | | | | | | | | | | |
| *Shake or vacuum rugs* | | | | | | | | | | | | | |
| *Sweep, then mop floor* | | | | | | | | | | | | | |
| *Check cleaning supplies* | | | | | | | | | | | | | |
| *Check grooming supplies* | | | | | | | | | | | | | |

better is *unsolicited* hugs and kisses. One day out of the blue my four-year-old said, "Mommy, I love you. I even love your skin." I still have warm feelings when I think about that. Do the same for your children. Give them those warm feelings without being asked. Let them know when a job is well done and brag about them to others. Chances are, if a child knows that you think she is a wonderful table setter, she will be consistent and won't let you down.

### 7. Have deadlines.

Knowing a task must get done by a certain time helps get kids going. For instance, if your son knows that he must make his bed before having breakfast, he can get to the task without a lot of extra dawdling. The incentive is built in; food for his hungry belly.

### 8. Set the example.

My father used to say that no man is a complete failure, he can always serve as a terrible example. The "do as I say, not as I do" theory gets you nowhere. If you want cooperation you have to be a good example yourself.

### 9. Give discipline for insubordination.

In its own way, punishment works as an incentive. The child does the chore because he or she doesn't want to face the punishment. The thing is, punishment is most effective when it is consistent, timely, and is related to the offense.

• Consistent means *always* sticking to the agreed upon course of action. Your children should be aware of what consequences they face if a chore is not done. Perhaps it will be a demerit, loss of a privilege, or loss of payment for the work. The key is consistency. If you dole out punishment half of the time and don't bother with it the other half, your child loses faith in what you say. He will continue to test you, knowing that half the time he can get away without doing his chore.

• Timeliness is important as well. Punishment must be meted out as soon after the time of the offense as possible. Otherwise issues become confused in the child's mind and the punishment loses its effectiveness. Mothers who threaten "Just wait until your father gets home!" are doing their children a disservice. In a child's mind, an early morning offense may easily be forgotten by dinner time. That's no time to bring it up again.

• Relate the form of punishment as closely as possible to the offense. Let's say that one of your daughter's weekly chores is to wash and vacuum the car. Her incentive for doing this is the privilege of using the car on Friday night. If she fails to clean the car a logical punishment would be that she loses the privilege of using the car. If your eight-year-old doesn't clean his room, a logical consequence would be that he couldn't have his friend sleep over that weekend.

It isn't always easy to tie punishment to the offense. In that case you need to choose a punishment that will still have meaning to them. If your computer hacker doesn't do his weekly chore, he may be forbidden to use the computer for two days. If he usually uses it every day, that will smart enough to make him think twice next time. Of course, when determining a punishment, you must decide on things that can actually be enforced. If you work late and your son will be alone, you have no way of knowing if he defies you and uses the computer anyway.

Remember too, what it is that you are trying to accomplish. You are not trying to make your children miserable, you are trying to teach them some responsibility and get some help around the house. It will help to keep those objectives in mind when your nerves are fraying.

Now, let's look at some specific things children can do to help with housework.

## LITTLE HELPING HANDS—WHAT THEY CAN DO

Here are some guidelines for age-appropriate capabilities. There are no hard-and-fast rules. You know your children better than anyone. You know what they are capable of and what would be too much. If you have concerns that a chore is too much for them, wait a year or two until they can handle it.

### Preschoolers

These of course are your neediest children. As yet unable to get their own apple juice or even brush their own teeth, they cannot be expected to scrub the bath or mop the floors (darn). They *can* however do *some* things. This is the ideal time to begin the process of establishing beneficial habits. You already have a couple of things going for you.

First, most little children love their mommies and want to spend virtually every waking moment in that blind spot just to Mom's side and slightly to the rear. This sort of closeness makes for lots of leg hugs as well as many mishaps when Mom accidentally bonks the little Clingon and sends him hurling.

Secondly, little children usually find adult behavior fascinating and have not yet caught on to the concept of "work." Consequently, some tasks seem to be games and they can't wait to shout "let me!"

Whatever you do, do not discourage their interest by insisting that they leave you alone while you do your work. Let them tag along as you do routine chores and when feasible, allow them to help.

Of course, tiny tots certainly should not be expected to do real work. However, they can do some small chores. For instance, they can begin to take responsibility for their own belongings. With your help they can:

- pick up and put away toys
- hang their coats on a low coat hook
- put shoes and boots away in the designated place
- reshelve books
- put dirty clothes in a laundry basket
- learn to make their beds (sort of, if you've made it easy enough)

As I said, they could do these things with *your* help. At this tender age children simply are not developmentally able to do chores on their own. Even if your little genius knows that his cars get stored in that special box on the shelf, he still can't be expected to clean up his room on a regular basis all by himself. He simply isn't able to make the connection necessary to understand exactly what else he needs to do to get the room to the point of "clean."

As for actual household cleaning tasks, they may do their child's version of the following:

## Dusting.

Though you may loathe this task, naive little ones think it's grand. If you give them a little cleaning cloth (even a washcloth) or a damp sponge, your little ones may surprise you. Of course, you must make sure they are dusting in safe areas, free of falling objects or breakable nicknacks. Horizontal surfaces such as low wood tables, coffee and end tables are good candidates. Dining room chairs with their spindle backs and low book shelves are other possibilities.

## Cleaning.

Another thing children love to do is use spray bottles. Of course, you wouldn't give them anything with a chemical cleaner in it. Their own spray bottle with plain water can keep them happy, helpful, and occupied for a long time. Let them clean low items, washable cabinets and doors, vinyl furniture, their potty chair and so forth. (Be sure they are old enough to understand they are not to touch *real* cleaners and keep the real cleaning products stored out of their reach.)

## Vacuuming/sweeping.

A child-size broom and vacuum (you may want to substitute a play lawnmower for a vacuum) are an investment that makes them feel "grown up" and keeps them happy while you do the real thing. Make sure they understand that they may only use their vacuum, not mommy's.

At this age, you should cultivate an appreciation for cleanliness and order. Point out how nice and comfortable the house is and how good you feel when things are tidy. Encourage them by adopting the "first we work and then we play" philosophy.

## TIPS FOR HELPING PRESCHOOLERS CONTRIBUTE

### Be prepared to help your children do their work.

Sometimes all that is needed is for you to be with them, keeping them company. Other times you will need to actually contribute to the work.

### Make the work interesting.

Make a game out of cleaning up the bedroom. You might call out something like this: "Simon says, 'Put away all the green toys first.' " Or, "I'll put away the hard toys while you put away the soft toys."

### Allow them to exercise decision-making skills by having a choice in the matter.

"Which would you rather put away, the building blocks or the art supplies?" Let them choose and you put away the other item.

### If you are not philosophically opposed, you may want to offer incentives.

It could be something as simple as giving a sticker each time a task is performed. A week's worth of stickers add up to a privilege or small toy, even an extra story one night at bedtime. Anytime they perform a simple task without being told to do it, they get *two* stickers.

### Don't spring work on children.

Always let them know that the work is coming, but don't harp on it.

### Don't give your children busy work.

They will see right through it and it will give them a bad attitude toward real work.

### Don't abruptly cut off play time.

Set an egg timer or verbally give them a ten-minute warning so they can finish up games and mentally prepare to stop the fun.

### Always let your children know you appreciate the contributions they make.

Here are a few more fun ideas for cleaning time:

- Pretend you are cleaning robots. Use funny voices and walk with stiff legs as you work.
- Try using an egg timer to help children distinguish small increments of time. Set it for two or three minutes and see how

much you can get done. They love the bell.

- Give your children fancy titles. "Supervising engineer for domicile clutteritis." Give them hats to go with the titles.
- Play the "what did you do?" game. Hide your eyes while your children put away three things. Now try to guess what they did. Next time, reverse the order and let them guess what you did.
- When cleaning their rooms, let your children wear their "Super Cleaner" capes. Just like other superheroes.

Though all of this interactive help may seem like a lot of work for you, consider it an investment; it will pay off in the future.

I said that little children are not capable of doing chores on their own. However, your child may be able to do simple tasks without being reminded, once the habits have become ingrained.

## ESTABLISHING HABITS IN YOUNG CHILDREN

The key to getting a task accomplished on a regular basis is to make it a habit. Some habits will be easier to develop than others. For instance, if you routinely walk into your house, remove your coat and immediately hang it on a coat rack, your child will likely imitate this and quickly begin to do it on his own. Rarely do I have to tell my four-year-old to hang up his coat.

More complex tasks, such as putting toys away, may be easier to instill if you link them to something else that he or she does regularly. Since little children thrive on routine, attaching beneficial habits to patterns and rules already distinctive to your family is a wonderful way of achieving your goal. For instance: "In our family, we have music practice each night after dinner." "In our family, it's the rule to put toys away before bathtime." Or, "Your older brother always feeds the dog as soon as he gets home from school." There is the one constant, the "anchor" if you will. For instance, dinner, bathtime, or coming home from school. Connecting a new habit with the established routine will link the two together as though they are genuinely related.

Introducing good routines at an early age will help the child accept them as givens, rather than choices — simply the way things are done around your house.

## HELP FROM SCHOOL-AGE CHILDREN

### Grade School Children

Grade school-age children will probably be some of your best help-ers. They are still young enough to want to spend time with you, yet they are old enough to begin to contribute. Obviously, first graders will not be able to help in the same way that eighth graders can, but they can take on more responsibility than younger siblings. You will have to use your own discretion regarding how much can be expected at what age.

Though your grade school-age children may now be more coordi-nated and better able to help, they will still likely need some assis-tance from you. Though they know perfectly well how to put their toys away, left to their own devices they forget. Don't be too impa-tient with them on this point. It's perfectly natural. Too often as parents we expect our children to be little adults. If you accept the fact that their forgetfulness is a normal facet of development, you will save yourself some frustration.

Ask them if they would like you to help them by reminding them of chores. Find out how they would like to be reminded. Should you tell them, or leave them a note? Some kids respond very well to written instructions. Some enjoy charts or other visual aids. Find out what they respond well to and do it that way. Offer thanks and praise through the same means.

And remember, siblings can be as different as night and day, so tune in to each one's unique personality.

Here are some ideas for tasks they can probably do.

### *Lower grade school (grades one through three).*

In addition to all the things mentioned for preschoolers, children in this age group are ready to do a better job of cleaning their rooms. They can:

- make their beds
- dust (please do not allow them to climb on things to reach high shelves, etc.)
- empty wastebaskets
- straighten drawers

- separate laundry (whites from colors, but nothing too complex)

In the rest of the house they can:

- help wash vegetables for dinner
- tear lettuce
- mix, stir and knead food
- clear their own place setting after dinner
- help with general pickup

### Middle grade school (grades four and five).

In addition to those things already mentioned, children in this age group should be able to take better care of their bedrooms. They should be doing a better job of making their beds now, dusting more thoroughly and keeping things off the floor.

Around the house they can also:

- dust
- polish (with care)
- sweep
- clean mirrors that they can easily reach

### Upper grade school (grades six through eight).

Children in this age bracket can do all of the previously mentioned as well as begin to pitch in with the actual cleaning. They can:

- do more dusting and polishing
- begin to scrub (within limits)
- help choose items at the grocery store
- help prepare the meal (again within guidelines)
- set the dinner table
- clear the table
- load and unload the dishwasher
- change bed linens
- sort and do laundry
- assist you with your other duties

### High School Kids

Though teenagers may be old enough to give you the most effective help, the question is, will they be there to give it? At this age, many children's lives become so busy that the amount of contributing they do at home is severely limited. After school activities, clubs, jobs, band practice and socializing are all very important at this age. While teenagers may be supremely capable of helping with housework, you may prefer for them to pursue their other interests at this time. This doesn't mean they are entirely excused (they should at the very least keep their own rooms tidy), but it may not be fair to expect them to give up extracurricular school and club activities in order to be of more help around the house. You will have to decide which you think is more beneficial for them. Perhaps they could still assist with a weekly chore or with a small daily chore. Of course, teenagers are more in need of pocket money than younger children, so continue to give them an allowance and offer incentives to make even *more* money by doing small jobs.

## THE WORK-OUTSIDE-THE-HOME HOMEMAKER

If you work outside your home, you probably have two professions. There's the one you get paid for and there's your "home" work. In most families with working women, the women still do the majority of the housework.

Not only is this double lifestyle exhausting, it's difficult. Very few people are able to keep up with the demands to the degree that they would like.

It is especially important for work-outside-the-home homemakers to get help from the family. It's also important to concentrate on the essentials. Don't get bogged down with guilt just because you haven't dusted the baseboards in two months.

Your two most likely main concerns are meal preparation and laundry. Here are a few tips.

• Keep meals simple. Some of the healthiest meals are those that require the least amount of trouble to prepare.

• Designate responsibility for each evening meal to a particular person. For instance, Dad cooks on Tuesdays and Thursdays. You cook on Mondays and Saturdays. Wednesday is leftovers night. You work together on that one. Friday you order in and Sunday everyone goes out to dinner.

• Assign your children specific jobs. For instance, if you have teens at home, they can begin meal preparations before you arrive home. Younger siblings can set the table, fill water glasses and set out condiments, while older siblings make a salad, wash and cut vegetables, or even put a chicken or roast in the oven.

• As for laundry, the rule of thumb should be that everyone who is old enough (teenagers) to do their own should be responsible for doing just that. Another approach would be to assign responsibility for particular categories of laundry to individual family members. There should be a clear understanding of *when* these chores are supposed to be done. For instance, you take responsibility for deli-cates and underwear. Dad washes work clothes. The kids wash towels and sheets. Individuals should be responsible for their own ironing.

Many of the other tips and ideas in this section will work well for you if you work outside the home. Scout out the ideas you like most and implement them as soon as possible.

## TWENTY FUN IDEAS TO HELP MOTIVATE KIDS TO WORK

If you are philosophically opposed to the electric cattle prod method and your knees are worn down to the bones from begging, try these cajoling methods, designed primarily for younger children:

• Using a magic marker, write a chore on an inflated balloon. Let the air out, toss several in a hat and allow the children to draw balloons. They must blow them back up to read the chore. Trades are OK if acceptable to both parties.

• Get everyone going on a team job such as tidying the living room by playing green light, red light. Mom or Dad call out "green light" and everyone scurries to do a task. Everyone must stop in their tracks when "red light" is called.

• Draw a vertical sketch of your house with the outside wall removed so that rooms can be seen. Hang it on the refrigerator or a magnetic board. Using little photo magnets of each family member, place people in the room for which they are responsible that week.

• Allow your child to contribute decorating ideas for his room. If he likes the way it is decorated, he may be more motivated to keep it clean.

• At dinner, pretend you are at a restaurant. Play music and have one child act as waiter, bringing plates of food to the table and filling water glasses. After the meal, the waiter clears the table. If he or she did a good job, leave a tip.

• To help young children learn to set the table, make a picture that shows a complete place setting as well as salt and pepper, butter, and whatever else you normally use. You could also use a picture from a magazine, if you can find a good one. Make sure dishes, silverware and napkins are stored down low so that little table setters can reach them.

• Let your nightly kitchen helper wear a fun apron and even a fancy hat. These could be items you purchase, or buy a plain apron and hat and decorate them together.

• Let each child pick out a special mug or tumbler that is just for them. That becomes theirs to use throughout the day rather than grabbing for a new one. Hang it from a rack or put it on a special shelf.

• In the playroom, hang a shoe bag and use pockets for small toys, toys missing parts, odds and ends.

• To make sure tricycles, cars, Bigwheels and so forth get put where they belong, create specific parking spaces. If these are stored in an outside place such as the garage, paint white or yellow lines on the floor to denote the spaces. If kept inside, use thick, brightly colored tape to make the lines.

• If a child is particularly moody one day, play the game of switching roles. He or she can be mommy or daddy and dole out the jobs such as "pick up your toys," "make the bed," "feed the fish" and so forth. They will get a kick out of it, and you may get some insight as to how they perceive *you*.

• Always do a chore (sometimes several times) with children before you expect them to do it on their own. Have the child verbally explain the job and go through the motions of doing it so that you know he thoroughly understands what it entails.

• Make sure some of the children's jobs are fun. For instance, picking flowers for arrangements, folding napkins in a fancy design, decorating oven-fresh cookies with candies and nuts, walking the dog, or reading to younger siblings.

• When cleaning a room, play the "outside-in" game. First they clean up things on the outside, then they work on drawers, cabinets and closets.

• To teach personal appearance principles, have Dad dress up as "Slobby Bobby." Let children give advice about what they need to do to be "Dapper Dan." You cover anything they may miss.

• For spring cleaning or pre-holiday cleaning, assign a child to be Sherlock Holmes. He goes through the house with magnifying glass in hand looking for mold and mildew, chipping paint, cobwebs and dirty trashcans. If he's old enough, let him jot down his room-by-room findings in a notebook or on a tape recorder. Otherwise, he reports to you after inspecting each room.

• Encourage participation in spring cleaning projects by promising something extra special when the work is through. Perhaps dinner at a fancy restaurant, a short camp out, a trip across the state, a day at an amusement park or something else.

• Let children play some of their favorite upbeat music while they work.

• Let children exercise decision-making skills as much as possible when you are doling out jobs. For instance, you may say to your teenage daughter, "There are three things that need to be done. The trash needs to be taken out, the dishwasher needs to be unloaded, and the living room needs to be dusted. I need you to do one. Which one would you prefer to do?"

• In addition to constructive household rules, have some silly ones. Anyone asking for extra treats must sing a little song or dance a little jig. Anyone late for dinner must stand at attention and say the Pledge of Allegiance. Such nonsense is fun for kids, makes everyone laugh, and establishes fun, unique traditions. Even when they eventually die out, they will be remembered fondly for years.

*Chapter Four*

# HELP FROM YOUR SPOUSE

As I see it, husbands can be classified in one of five basic groups when it comes to helping around the house.

## 1. The King of the Castle

This sort of man still considers housework to be "woman's work." It's an affront to his masculinity just to ask him to consider washing the dishes, changing the baby or vacuuming the living room.

Fortunately, these men seem to be fewer and farther between these days, but there are still some holdouts. If this describes your husband, start fasting and praying because this sort of husband will be the hardest to deal with.

## 2. The Pinch Hitter

This is the sort of man who will pitch in with last-minute details. He'll pick up the living room when you suddenly remember that company is coming in five minutes. Occasionally, he'll even clean the kitchen without being asked. He's better than the king of the castle, but you can't count on him to get specific things done on a regular basis. If this describes your husband, you will have your work cut out for you, but you can definitely make some progress with this guy.

## 3. The Pooped-Out Workaholic

This sort of husband either works oodles of overtime or has a back-breaking job. The fact that he is not home much, or is usually exhausted or in pain precludes him helping. Even if he had a willing attitude, his help would not be readily available. If this describes your husband, you will have to be very patient.

## 4. The Fair Player

This sort of man has a good understanding of what it takes to run a home and care for children all day. He is much more likely than the others to help. All you need to do is determine a reasonable distribution of the work. If this is the sort of husband you have, you are very fortunate indeed.

## 5. The Original Felix Unger

This dreamboat insists that you relax with a cool drink while he beats the rugs, bathes the children, prepares dinner and chills the wine. Of course, we all know that Felix Unger exists only in playwright Neil Simon's fertile imagination. Still, I included this category because with five and a half billion men on the planet, I figured that there is a statistical chance that there actually is *one* real life Felix Unger out there.

## TO HELP OR NOT TO HELP

Whether you're dealing with the king of the castle or a pinch hitter, you want one thing: more help from your husband! The best way to get his help is to convince him that you actually do need it.

I think some husbands are under the mistaken impression that housekeeping and mothering are easy and come very naturally to women. While that may be true for some women, others struggle tremendously with these responsibilities.

A few years ago, I saw a television program that featured homemakers who felt unappreciated by their spouses. One woman lamented the amount of work involved in running a household with four children. Her husband was a blue collar worker who put in hard labor all day. From his perspective, she had it easy. He just couldn't understand what was so difficult about throwing some clothes into a washing machine.

If you lay around all day while he works (or if your husband just *thinks* you do), then he is likely to resent it if you ask for his help when he gets home. If on the other hand, he understands that you too have been working hard, his sense of fair play should come to the fore. He will be far more willing to help out if he sees the situation as a team effort where you both pull your own weight.

If at all possible, expose your husband to your daily routine. Take a few days off and visit a friend or relative in another state. Let him have a chance to take care of the kids, do all the housework, and prepare all the meals. That ought to do it.

Here are some ideas. First, some general tips to keep in mind, then some specific ideas. I make no guarantees, I only make suggestions.

For your own peace of mind:

## Do not make a contest of your lives.

You are not competing to see who works the hardest or accomplishes the most. Don't make the mistake of taking a "woe is me" attitude about your situation. You and your husband have a *joint* interest in your home, your children, your life together. Don't try to "outdo" him with stories about how difficult your life is. Chances are he has plenty of those stories from work himself. Men usually aren't as verbal about their problems, but that doesn't mean they don't exist.

## Recognize that your perspectives differ.

I think much of the frustration that women experience regarding housework is due to the fact that their vision for the home differs so much from that of their husbands. Chances are, you don't even realize this. You simply assume that he wants what you want. Wrong. If he doesn't even notice the new curtains in the living room, how is he to notice that the shelves need dusting? It's not necessarily that he doesn't care (although that could be true in some cases), it's that his focus is elsewhere. While you may be more in tune to the house, he may be more in tune to his job or other responsibilities. This does not make him a louse. You will save yourself a lot of aggravation if you understand this.

## Believe in his goodwill.

I believe that most husbands *want* to please their wives. Don't assume that he is a lazy slug who enjoys seeing you slave away. After all, you married him. How bad can he be?

To increase the likelihood of his help:

### Keep things simple in every way.

If you want help, you will have to make jobs palatable. If you were to ask your husband to dust the living room and it took him an hour and a half because you have so much clutter—eighty-seven tiny thimbles resembling English country cottages, all forty-seven decorative plates in the "This is Elvis" collection, thirty-three frogs hopping all over tables and shelves, every Hummel figurine ever issued, and an extensive collection of antique porcelain dolls—well, what do you expect? The poor exhausted man will probably never help again. If giving in to your own weakness (being an unrelenting clutterbug) complicates household chores, be prepared to take responsibility yourself. It's really not fair to expect a spouse or children to have to suffer for your idiosyncrasy.

### Have a place for everything.

This point has been made before but it's important enough to make again. If you haven't got a specific "home" for each of your possessions, your husband won't be much help in keeping things orderly. It will be easier for your whole family to cooperate if every item has an easily distinguishable home. Otherwise, odds and ends tend to get shoved into the nearest available drawer, closet or cupboard. Once you do assign items specific places, label closets, cupboards, shelves and drawers to help your family members help you.

### Don't nag.

I know you want to. I personally agree with the philosophy that if only husbands would do what they are supposed to do, like take out the trash, then their wives wouldn't ever nag them. It seems perfectly reasonable to me. However, nagging only makes them feel resentful. That will *not* help your cause. In addition, feeling that you must tell him the same thing over and over makes you feel resentful, not to mention angry. Once you have agreed on specific tasks for him to do, do not remind him. Let him deal with the natural consequence of leaving the job undone.

### Be certain that what you ask is fair.

It's really not fair to expect a husband who has worked twelve hours to come home and do half of the housework because you don't like doing it. You have to do your part and he has to do his part, but neither one of you needs to do 80 percent.

## Try These Suggestions for Getting Help

### Communicate your needs.

Come right out and let him know that you are falling behind and that you need his help. Explain that you will be less stressed and grouchy if you get some help.

### Give him choices.

For instance, you may say something like this, "There are three weekly chores that I am most concerned with. They are getting the laundry done, doing the grocery shopping, and ironing your work clothes for the week. I can do two of those. Which would you be able to do?"

### Do jobs together.

If possible, think of things you can do together. This helps bolster the feeling of being a team and working for a common cause. Ideas include: he sorts, folds and puts away clothes while you iron; he unloads the dishwasher while you clear the counters; he dusts the living room while you vacuum; or he clears the table and puts left-overs away while you wash the dishes. Try a variety of options until you hit on those that work.

### When asking him to do a job, be specific about what the job entails.

If you ask him to clean the living room, you may be very frustrated about the things left undone. His definition of clean may vary from yours. If you specifically need him to dust and vacuum, make that clear up front or he may only do a general pickup.

### Be careful about the way you ask for help.

For instance, rather than say, "Could you take out the garbage?" say, "Would you take out the garbage?" Of course he *could* take out the garbage, but what you really want to know is if he is *willing* to take it out. The second way of asking gives him a choice.

### Offer trades if you think he would like them.

For instance you could say, "If you will help clean the kitchen every night after dinner, I'll take over paying the bills." Or, "If you will be responsible for dinner on Tuesday and Thursday nights, I'll vacuum and wash your car each weekend." Or even, "If you will get the kids ready for bed every night, I'll tuck them in and read them some bedtime stories."

### Ask him for his suggestions.

Let him suggest what he can do. He will be more likely to follow through if he makes the decision about what he does.

### Always have a day off together.

I know this is often difficult, but even God took a day off. Give your husband an incentive to help by arranging your schedule so that one day a week can truly be a work-free day together. For instance, Sunday would be a logical choice for many people. Rather than cooking up a feast, relax. For breakfast everyone has cereal instead of bacon and eggs. Go out for lunch. Dinner is something simple you prepared the day before. Perhaps Saturday's leftovers, some simple sandwiches, or even a pizza delivered to your door. If you plan ahead a bit, you can really be "off" on your day off.

### List everything that needs to be done, if you face major resistance.

It will be a lot of work for you, but it could pay off in the end if it brings him around. Write down all the work that is necessary to keep the home orderly and things running smoothly. Do this room by room. Faced with this, a reasonable person could hardly refuse to help.

### If all else fails, you may want to do as one woman did.

When she couldn't seem to get any cooperation from her spouse, she took to doing things only for herself. She washed and ironed only her own clothes, cooked meals for only herself, picked up only her own messes and so forth. Her reluctant spouse got the message and began carrying his own weight. Their relationship improved immensely. She no longer felt that she was taken for granted and he enjoyed her more relaxed attitude. They found they enjoyed doing things together. The teamwork brought them closer and gave them a better appreciation of each other. Because jobs got done faster, they had more "fun" time together. Her scheme turned out better than she dared to dream. Wouldn't it be wonderful if things could work so well for you?

Good luck!

———————

*Chapter Five*

# BEATING THE HIGH PRICE OF PROCRASTINATION

*Never put off until tomorrow what you can do the day after tomorrow.*
—*Mark Twain*

It's 9 P.M. and the dinner dishes still haven't been done, but your favorite television program is about to come on. Besides, you're tired. You can always do them in the morning.

If this sounds even *vaguely* familiar, then you know what happens next. It's 7 A.M. and everyone is screaming for breakfast. You can't get to it because you're elbow deep in last night's spaghetti feast. You think you've discovered some sort of new bonding material, because you're sure you'll never dislodge Uncle Guido's recipe for alfredo sauce from every dish, pot and countertop in the house. In the meantime, the kids have grabbed the closest junk food and they're all asking why their lunch boxes are empty. It's time to catch the bus.

Something like this has probably happened to everybody at least once. For some of us, dozens of times. For some crazy reason, we don't do what we know we should do and we always wind up paying the price.

Figure it this way: first there's the price you pay for the guilt feelings. The dishes are calling. You try to ignore them, but the knowledge that spaghetti sauce is becoming one with your stoneware haunts you. Then, there's the self-loathing. While you try to ignore the calling dishes, you can't ignore your own inner voice. You know, the one that calls you a lazy slug and other charming epithets.

Even your subconscious pays the price. That night you dream giant meatballs are chasing you. You're stuck in a quicksand of spaghetti sauce. Somebody throws you a rope; no, it's a piece of crusty, dried up spaghetti. It snaps, you sink. Ciao.

Starting a new day with work left over from the previous day immediately puts you at a disadvantage. You feel as though you're playing catch up all day. That nagging feeling of guilt and inadequacy haunts you. You mentally berate and batter yourself and wind up exhausted. And for what? Simply for putting off a job you had to do *sometime* anyway. Ugh!

If the scenario above sounds all too familiar, then you have plenty of company. Millions of people count themselves as procrastinators. Some of these have resigned themselves to their fate. They even make jokes about it in an attempt to excuse themselves or assuage their guilt. Of course, we all procrastinate sometimes, and sometimes with very good reason. But chronic procrastination ruins lives. You have got to overcome it.

## CAN A PERSON REALLY OVERCOME PROCRASTINATION?

Yes. I'm living proof. And my history is a long one. I was one of those kids who invariably put off doing the science project until the night before it was due. I envied the kids who managed to have scale prototypes two weeks before the assignment deadline. And my weekends were never any fun. Racked with guilt, I worried from Friday afternoon until 9 P.M. Sunday night (straight through the *Wonderful World of Disney*), when I finally got around to homework. I even procrastinated when getting up for school. I was chronically late.

I can't tell you exactly when it was that I conquered procrastination. There were no fireworks or presidential proclamations to announce the news. I know I didn't perform any death-defying feats or win a million dollars for my effort. What I do know is that it didn't happen overnight, but my *attitude* did change that quickly. Once I made up my mind that I would not tolerate this quirk in my personality any longer, I was a new person. I simply had no choice but to plow ahead and get things done.

It's a good thing I did too, because if I hadn't, I would *still* be a slave to my home and I would be miserable.

## PROCRASTINATOR'S POTPOURRI

Sometimes it helps a person to be aware of what it is that they are putting off. Based on my experience, I have been able to determine three distinct procrastination personalities. There may be more and there may even be scientific names for them, but I'm no Sigmund Freud. All I know is what I have encountered. See if you fall into one of these categories.

## The General Procrastinator

The problem — this person procrastinates in every area of her life. She has as much difficulty filing a report for work as she does changing from screens to storm windows at home. She has no prejudices or biases. Everything gets put off for as long as possible.

Possible causes — she has trouble with organization and time management. She hasn't learned to effectively juggle all the demands that life heaps on her. It's easy to keep putting things off because she really has no system for getting them done.

The solution — if this describes your situation, take heart in the fact that you have already started the process for overcoming procrastination. By purchasing and reading this book, you have made a commitment to yourself to get things under control. If you haven't already done so, go back now to chapter two and devise a reasonable schedule for getting your housekeeping chores accomplished. By getting housework under control you will take a giant leap in overcoming procrastination. Doing so will likely lead to mastery in other areas as well.

## The Specific Procrastinator

The problem — this person has several areas of her life under control. There are just a few specific things that she continues to put off. She can't understand how she can do so well with some things and fail so miserably with others.

Possible causes — there are lots of possibilities. Perhaps she is in a power struggle with someone in one particular area and she exercises her power by causing delays. Perhaps someone else benefits from her procrastination, such as a parent who is able to continue as the authority figure by scolding her or perhaps a spouse who is able to rescue her and therefore has a feeling of being needed. She may not even realize that other people are benefiting. Of course, it could be that she loathes that particular task.

The solution — if this describes your situation, you need to deal with the underlying conflict first. You are using the procrastination to abet the other problem. Once the underlying problem is solved, you will be free to stop procrastinating. If the procrastination is due to a desire to avoid an undesirable job, then try a variety of bribes to get yourself going. Promise yourself a special treat or luxury when the job is completed. Make the work atmosphere as pleasant as possible. Play music, simmer potpourri. When possible, employ someone *else* to do the job.

## The Perfectionist Procrastinator

The problem — many people who put things off do so because they are perfectionists. It's actually their pursuit of the impossible that causes them to procrastinate. They may not even realize it, but subconsciously they put off completing projects because they know they'll never get them right.

Possible causes — sometimes these people have had parents who were hard to please. No matter how well his child did a chore, the father always found fault with the tiniest detail. Never did he praise all the things the child did right. Consequently, the perfectionist procrastinator only focuses on the negative. They are forever haunted by the idea that they can do better.

The solution — if this describes your situation, come to grips with the fact that you are not perfect. Take comfort in knowing that nobody else is, either. Recognize the fact that you do not have to be perfect to be successful. Perfectionists *aren't* successful because they sabotage themselves too much with their unrealistic expectations. Successful people *are not* perfectionists. Besides, if you don't try something because you are afraid of failing, then you have already failed.

I used to be a perfectionist procrastinator. Here are two personal examples of how I learned to free myself from perfectionism.

### *What Margie Pepper taught me.*

When I was in the sixth grade, I had a classmate named Margie Pepper. Margie taught me a great lesson about life. To this day I often think about the simple example that Margie set that had such a tremendous effect on my life and my enjoyment of life. What Margie taught me was to be free of perfectionism. How could an eleven-year-old girl teach such an important lesson? Actually it was very simple. She taught me by her own example.

Margie and I had an art class together. Each time we met, the teacher had some sort of assignment for us. Sometimes the assignment could be finished with time to spare.

One day, as I repeatedly started and then trashed my creations, struggling in vain to get them perfect, I noticed that Margie had not only completed the assignment, but had actually done a few paintings with the leftover time. The serene, satisfied expression on her face as she held up and admired another painting really gave me cause to think. Here she was with no less than four completed projects and I didn't even have one. What was it about her? Looking at her projects, I wouldn't have called any of them exactly *perfect*, but they were at least *complete*. There was no mistaking that. She was leaving class that day with a satisfied sense of completion and accomplishment (not to mention four things to show to her mother) and all I had were empty hands and a stomach in knots from feelings of inadequacy. I decided that I would be more satisfied with a complete, albeit imperfect, project than a nonexistent one. I finally realized that perfection wasn't for humans and I wasn't getting anywhere in my pursuit of it. After that day I enjoyed art class as I never had before. I took a relaxed attitude, *enjoyed* doing the assignments, and then proudly took home completed projects every time.

Please do not misunderstand me, I am not endorsing slovenliness or sloppiness. What I am saying is that perfection is an unattainable goal. Do the best that you are *capable* of doing, and be satisfied. Consider the biblical concept "Finishing is better than starting." Anybody can start anything. I had started dozens of things and hated myself for not being able to perfectly complete them. When I learned to free myself of perfectionism I became a finisher. It's been many years since all of this took place and I still think of Margie fondly.

### In pursuit of perfect penmanship — what Mom taught me.

Both of my parents have beautiful penmanship. The Palmer method of penmanship was taught by my second grade teacher, a nun. The nuns at St. Aidan's took a very serious interest in penmanship and more specifically the correct and excellent pursuit of proper Palmer penmanship. Consequently, I also have nice penmanship.

> Sometimes it's hard to know who you are. There are so many facets to all of us. Don't consider yourself coal just because you missed a deadline. You're a diamond in the rough. Soon you will sparkle brilliantly.

Like any child, I learned more from what my parents did, the examples that they set, than what they said. One thing I noticed about my mother when I was young, was that she practiced writing before she actually did it. That is, she would wave the pen around above the paper a few times before she would begin to write. Presumably to practice the motions. If things didn't turn out as well as she liked when she did write, she would toss the paper and start over.

What this conveyed to me was that one's penmanship must be perfect to be acceptable. That example, coupled with the nuns' passion for Palmer penmanship, nearly sent me to an insane asylum. I'm kidding of course. What I mean is that I became obsessed with perfect penmanship. I mistakenly thought it was possible. I drove myself crazy doing and redoing assignments that had the tiniest flaw. Eventually I began procrastinating. I put off doing assignments, knowing that I would never get the penmanship right.

Corresponding by mail literally became an impossibility because I was rarely able to perfectly complete a letter. This pursuit of perfect penmanship left me with feelings of anxiety and frustration. I finally gave up corresponding with people by mail. I'd wind up with a pile of balled up sheets of paper all around me on the floor, and no letter, every time.

Fortunately, somewhere along the line (probably after the Margie Pepper revelation) I had the good sense to realize that it is profoundly preferable to mail a letter with a few mistakes in it, than to lose touch with people one cares about. My friends would probably tell you what terrible penmanship I have. You know what? I don't care! I'm free from the pursuit of perfection and I actually get things mailed and you know what else? People write back! It's great.

Whatever your procrastination potential, you could probably spend years (not to mention thousands of dollars) in therapy trying to analyze your problems. Don't let your natural desire to understand this problem be another form of procrastination! Instead, start looking for solutions. Concentrate less on the why you are doing it and more on how to accomplish the task.

I found that if I could manage to take just one step toward my goal, I was practically halfway there. The doing wasn't nearly as difficult or worrisome as the not doing. When I took the first step, I was poised for the second. When I took the second step, I was poised for the third. It was a natural progression. Once I got started, things tended to fall into place much better than my worrying had anticipated.

Of course, you may sometimes have a valid reason for putting something off. Perhaps you are short on some needed tools or information to get the job done. Beware, however, that putting off getting those tools or information is just another form of procrastinating.

## CONDITIONING OR EXERCISING YOUR "DO IT NOW" MUSCLE

Nobody in their right mind would try to bench press three hundred pounds without prior preparation. Weight trainers tell athletes to start out small and, by consistent repetition, build their muscles, periodically adding small amounts of weights until finally they can bench press their goal.

My advice is the same. Don't try to tackle every area of your life (that three hundred pounds) right off the bat. *Build some muscle.* Start out with one or two small, specific things. Repeat these consistently until they are mastered. You will likely find other things falling into place as you change your attitudes and successfully complete tasks.

By the way, you probably learned in your high school psychology class, as did I, that habits take a minimum of twenty-one days to establish. So don't expect an overnight conversion. Give yourself a fair shake and discipline yourself to stay with it for a month. That's not so much to ask from yourself. You can do it. You know you can.

## STEPS FOR CONQUERING PROCRASTINATION

Here now, are the steps to follow to help yourself overcome procrastination.

### 1. Create a sense of urgency about the problem.

It's not cute or funny, it's rotten. See it for what it really is: a life-threatening, time-robbing, success-stealing, career-ruining rat! It's you or the rat. Which is it going to be?

### 2. Know your exact destination.

When you get in your car to drive to the grocery store, you know exactly what your destination is. You get into your car and you drive the most direct route. You arrive at your destination *as expected.*

To overcome procrastination, you need to have a clear picture of where you are going. Without a specific destination, you won't know which route to take or even whether you've arrived. Decide what it is that you want. Be specific. Don't say, "I want to stop procrastinating on housework." Say, "I've decided to stop procrastinating on making my bed. I'll make it every morning before I leave the house for work." Now you have a concrete goal and a plan for getting it done.

### 3. Do the preparatory work.

Prepare yourself in every possible way so that your success is likely. That means, have the necessary information and tools to do the job. If you constantly put off doing the laundry, one reason may be that your laundry room is not set up efficiently. If you always seem to be out of detergent, if your dryer is broken half the time, if hidden crayons melt all over your best clothes, it's no wonder that you put it off. The negative experiences have set up this unpleasant association with doing the laundry. You're not unusual; anyone would feel that way!

If you have your tools set up so that this task can be accomplished with the least amount of trouble, it's more likely to get done in a timely fashion. Do the preparation so that the real task can be done swiftly and easily.

### 4. Proceed.

Now that you know where you are going and you have your tools, you must proceed to your destination. You don't wish yourself to the grocery store; you get in the car and drive yourself. So, get into gear and start moving. Take action. Do whatever is necessary so that you will actually begin the process. (Tips for getting yourself to take action follow.)

## 5. Review your progress.

Did you arrive at your destination? If not, why? If what you did didn't work effectively, try something else. If every time you tried to drive to work you ran into dead ends and detours, would you give up? Of course not. You'd try a different route. Do that here as well. Keep trying until you *get* there. If you're not succeeding, assess the reason. If, despite your clearly defined goal, the bed still is not getting made, figure out why. Is it very time consuming or difficult to make? What can you do to make it easier on yourself? Move it away from the wall? Get rid of the frills? What about getting up three minutes earlier?

## 6. Be proud of yourself.

When you successfully reach your destination, revel in the feelings of accomplishment. Feel good right down to your toes. You need to establish a pleasurable feeling to getting things done. It must be a stronger motivation than the reason for putting them off. Remember the pain, embarrassment, frustration and self-hatred that accompanied procrastination. Now associate the feelings of accomplishment, well-being, control and self-mastery to the completion of tasks. Really work at this so your mind is conditioned to this attitude.

## TAKING ACTION — TIPS TO HELP YOURSELF GET GOING

All the advice in the world is really useless if you don't get moving. And of course, nobody can do that for you. If you really have trouble getting going, prime yourself for action. When I was really struggling with this problem, I always came back to the question, "Why don't I just *proceed?*" I found four ways of motivating myself to take action. Figure out which works best for you.

## 1. Guilt worked very well for me.

If I was standing in the midst of a messy house I'd ask myself, "Is this really the kind of person you want to be? Do you really want to live like this? You don't have to be this way. What if a friend dropped by right now? Would you face embarrassment and open the door or would you pretend you weren't home and miss a nice visit?"

Or, perhaps some guilt on behalf of my family: "Is this the kind of example you want to set for your kids? Do you want them to be procrastinators also? Why do they have to pay the price of your procrastination? You keep saying you're going to change, but when? How much of your life will you let slip by before you grab control? Last year, didn't you wish you could just get yourself to do something? A whole year has passed. Do you want to be wishing the same thing a year from now? Won't you feel ashamed if you do?"

Then I'd project my future if I remained a procrastinator. "Do you want to wind up eighty-four years old, sitting in your rocking chair, wondering what if? What if you had actually followed through? What if you had finished projects and goals?" That was probably the scariest thought I could have had, that I would end my life wondering what if?

If this works for you, really pile it on until you feel so ashamed you never want to feel that way again. If that doesn't get you going, I don't know what will.

## 2. Concentrate on the pleasant feelings associated with completing the task.

Some people benefit from this approach. There must be a time in your life when you didn't procrastinate on something. Can you dredge up the feelings you experienced at that time? The satisfaction, sense of self-discipline, the peace of mind and so forth. There's nothing wrong with wanting to feel those. If it works better for you than guilt, then concentrate on your goal and the good feelings that accompany reaching it. Remember your past successes and dwell on them. Relive the good feelings until they are so real, you want them again. You know you can feel that way again, if you will take action. In your mind's eye, imagine yourself as though your task has been completed. See how happy and comfortable you feel.

## 3. The reward system.

Many people can motivate themselves with the promise of a reward for a job well done. If you would like to try this, make a clear distinction as to what problem you will be conquering and what exactly the reward will be. For instance, let's say you wanted to get

> The goal of procrastination is to put things off. Yet, the end result — the achievement of that goal — is not a victory. Procrastination is a self-defeating goal.

into the habit of making your bed every morning before you left for work. Promise yourself that if you do it every day this week, you'll get a reward. The reward is entirely up to you, but you should decide before you begin. It's helpful to know what it is you are working for. Also, the reward doesn't have to mean an expenditure of money. It could be something like a luxurious, two-hour bubble bath while your spouse watches the kids.

### 4. The five-minute deal.

If you are really having a hard time beginning something, try this. Let's say the living room is an absolute wreck. It's so overwhelming, you don't know where to begin. Make a deal with yourself to work for just five minutes (or ten). Do as much as you can in that amount of time. If, when the time is up you want to stop, do so. At least you've gotten something accomplished. Many times however, you will find that just moving, getting into gear and doing something will be enough motivation to finish up. When you see how much you accomplished in just five minutes, you'll probably tell yourself that it won't take that much longer to finish. This is a great trick when the whole family pitches in.

Probably a combination of all four of these strategies would work best.

## Chopping Down the Oak Tree — Attacking the Project Step by Step

An oak tree isn't felled with one swing of the axe and most jobs aren't completed in one step either. Many goals seem overwhelming when you see them as one big, looming task. In fact, that's exactly how most procrastinators see things. Because they tend to put things off to the very last minute, the whole thing must be completed in one seemingly endless session. (My science projects.)

To successfully avoid the feeling of being overwhelmed, you must approach the task as a series of smaller tasks. Each goal achieved brings you closer to your final destination. Use the steps outlined below. Here's an example.

Let's imagine that you have decided to reorganize your kitchen. Let's look at how we can chop down this oak tree, one swing at a time.

Get out a pencil, paper and calendar to map out your plans.

### Step 1. Create the mindset.

Every time you set a goal, you should make your sense of urgency so strong that you literally cannot accept any other outcome. You have made up your mind to do this and you will see that it is done. There are no other possibilities. Procrastination itself should be viewed as more of a problem than the inconvenience of accomplishing the task.

### Step 2. Know your exact destination.

Determine your outcome. What is the end result of this project? For instance, you want a better organized kitchen. Exactly *what* do you want to be better organized? List things specifically:

a. The refrigerator. Group categories of food in the refrigerator, using baskets to organize and contain.

b. Reorganize the cabinets located near the stove. Find suitable locations for pots and pans, cooking utensils, storage containers, cooking spices, oils and sauces.

c. Reorganize the cabinets located near the dishwasher. Use the space more efficiently to store dishes, glasses and silverware.

d. Clear the counters of items that are not used at least twice a week.

### Step 3. Determine your completion date.

Look over your schedule, and eliminate the days you will not be able to work on the reorganizing project. Mondays, Wednesdays and Fridays are bad for you. That leaves you four days a week. But, you'd really rather not work on Sundays either. That leaves you with Tuesdays, Thursdays and Saturdays. Afternoons are busy for you, so, realistically, you only have three mornings a week.

You will be having house guests coming in three weeks. You don't want to be working on this right up to the last minute. You decide to project two weeks from tomorrow as your completion date. That means that you will have to complete your project in six sessions. Is that realistic?

### Step 4. *Do the preparatory work.*

You've already determined your exact destination, and in doing so, outlined a plan for getting there. Now you need supplies. You know you want to purchase baskets for use in the refrigerator and wire drawers that roll out to organize the pots. You will shop for supplies on the first day of your six sessions. That will leave you with five sessions to complete your project by your own deadline.

You could stop there, or if you like, you could break the project down further. (I suggest you do, but some may find this too detailed for their temperaments.) For example:

a. Plan to work on the refrigerator organization the second session.
b. On the next, you work on the countertops.
c. The fourth session you work on the cabinets located by the dishwasher.
d. The fifth session you begin work on the cabinets located near the stove. This is the biggest part of the project and if it requires more time, you still have one more session allotted on your project calendar.

### Step 5. *You've got a great plan. Proceed.*

### Step 6. *Review your progress.*

Did you reach your destination? Did you complete the kitchen reorganization project in the time planned? If not, why not?

### Step 7. *If so, revel in the good feelings!*

And if not, determine how you can finish the goal; just because you didn't complete the reorganization by the original date doesn't mean you should abandon the project.

See how breaking things down into specific little jobs makes the whole seem more manageable? Of course, things don't always go smoothly. The store could be out of a needed supply or you could come down with the flu. But, having a plan will take out many of the surprises and put you in control. With this plan, you should easily meet your goal. *Cut your oak tree one swing at a time.*

## Some Suggestions

*Don't overburden yourself by trying to overcome procrastination in every area of your life at one time.*
Pick one or two specific things and work on them. Other things will fall into place. Start with something relatively small. For instance, make your bed every morning, or make sure the dinner dishes are done before you go to bed at night.

*Use your schedule to help keep yourself on track.*

*Be reasonable with yourself.*
It's not reasonable to bound up from the dinner table with the last bite of food still in your mouth and do the dishes. It is reasonable to get them done by some other marker. For instance, get them done before you go out, watch television, or certainly before you go to bed.

*Don't be a "yes man."*
Become a "no ma'am." Many people procrastinate because they feel overwhelmed. They never turn down a request. If you have difficulty saying no to requests, let me assure you of one thing. Anyone asking for help to coordinate something would much rather have you say no, than to have you agree, only to do a sloppy job or miss the deadline completely. If you can't imagine yourself saying no, practice. Create a few imaginary scenarios and practice your response. (It doesn't matter if this seems silly to you; all the great speakers practice when they're alone. How do you think they got to be great?) With enough prior practice, you may be able to gracefully deny a surprise request.

*If you find yourself wanting to put off a task, face up to it.*
Usually we just try to bury the guilt feelings. Instead, admit to it. Say something like this, "OK, I'm going to procrastinate on this now because _____ (fill in the excuse of your choice) and I know I will pay the price later." At least by making a conscious choice you may be able to forego some of the guilt and maintain your power.

## CONSISTENCY WILL TIP THE SCALES

If you have been procrastinating most of your life, you will probably find a victory very sweet. When you are able to successfully complete any task that you would normally put off, then you have successfully beat the procrastination bug one time.

Now, a warning, and this is not meant to be negative. While every victory is worthy of celebration, you have to remember that you have to have *many* victories to really tip the scales in your favor so that getting things done in a timely fashion becomes a way of life for you.

Think of a scale. With no weight on either side, the scales are balanced. Now, let's put a bunch of grapes on one side. It tips the scales drastically. Let's imagine that the bunch of grapes represents all the procrastinating that you do. Now imagine that you have a victory. One grape is removed from the bunch and put on the other side of the scale. That one grape is not enough to outweigh the bunch on the other side. But, with every victory you remove one grape from the bunch and put it on the other side. At some point, the scales are evenly matched; you could go either way. Eventually, the entire bunch has been moved, one grape at a time, so that the scales are now heavily tipped in your favor. At that point, the likelihood of procrastinating is greatly diminished.

## THE END (OF PROCRASTINATING)

Procrastination is no longer an issue in my life. Amazing, considering it was once a huge issue. The thing is, I don't even consider procrastinating about things anymore. It really doesn't even occur to me. Putting something off now represents so much pain and inconvenience, I simply can't allow myself to procrastinate.

I like being the sort of person who can get things done. I would like for you to derive strength from the knowledge that I succeeded in overcoming this problem. That means it *can* be done. Remember that if things get tough. I did it, you can too.

Oh, and as to that quotation by Mark Twain, "Never put off until tomorrow what you can do the day after tomorrow," I find it an interesting comment from a very accomplished man. I for one am glad that Mr. Twain did not take his own advice. Had he, he would have forever remained Samuel Clemens and we would not have the legacy of his literature and his wit. Lucky for us, he adhered more closely to Ben Franklin's famous quotation, "Never put off until tomorrow what you can do today." I have to wonder though, how many other would-be Mark Twains were stopped by procrastination. Don't let procrastination stop you from following your dreams!

*Chapter Six*

# THE CLUTTER SHUFFLE (IT'S NOT A DANCE)

*"Clutter is anything you own which does not enhance your life on a regular basis."*
—*Pam McClellan*

Have you ever known anyone who was a collector? I've known people who collected mushrooms, frogs, pigs, spoons, thimbles, plates, butterflies, hippopotamuses, beer cans, and even salt and pepper shakers. These collections seem harmless, even cute to begin with, but they defy all laws of nature in how quickly they grow.

Friends and relatives are more than happy to contribute to the collection by way of birthday presents, Christmas presents, and "I fell down and broke my leg so I got you this" presents. Any vacationing tourist who spots a pig that sports "Florida" on its side feels compelled, even duty bound, to get it for their pig-collecting friend. The pigs become a major topic of conversation and when the friend's name is mentioned, a stranger on the other side of the room is heard to say, "Oh yeah, she's the one with the pigs." The price of notoriety.

The pigs are happy pigs, sad pigs, sleeping pigs, or mommy pigs nursing baby pigs. There are dancing pigs with hats and tourist pigs wearing Bermuda shorts and sunglasses. The pigs even have names and are introduced when company comes. "This one's Porky and this one's Oink. Over there are Porkchop and Ima."

The collection grows and grows and pretty soon people with cameras are paying admission to view the assortment and the media is calling for interviews. It gets to the point that even though the family is sick and tired of pigs, they are tolerated like a pesky relative. After all, what does one *do* with a collection like this? It's so big. You can't just get rid of it, can you?

Collections are one of the more notorious and easily distinguished forms of clutter. That's because they generally exist for no other purpose than amusement or display. But, even if you do not have a collection per se, you are still not off the hook. Chances are, you are still a collector of clutter because it takes so many forms. Let's see if you recognize any of your own clutter by taking this quiz.

## YOUR CLUTTER QUOTIENT
Answer yes or no.

Do you have clothes hanging in your closet that are too small, too big, out of style, need repair, or that for some other reason you don't wear?

_____ yes  _____ no

Do you save broken gadgets, appliances and electronics, thinking that you may be able to fix them someday?

_____ yes  _____ no

Do you save magazines and newspapers that you don't have time to read now?

_____ yes  _____ no

Do you save dozens of empty pickle jars, bread sacks or brown grocery bags because they may come in handy?

_____ yes  _____ no

Do you have a cache of unusable odds and ends? For example keys from former residences, old safe deposit boxes, or the trunk of your first car.

_____ yes  _____ no

Do you hang on to things for sentimental reasons?

_____ yes  _____ no

Do you have several unfinished hobby projects hanging around?

_____ yes    _____ no

Do you save junk mail (catalogs) to browse through later?

_____ yes    _____ no

Do your kitchen counters look like a testimonial for "Gadgets R Us"?

_____ yes    _____ no

Do you tend to stock up on things? (Thirty-six bottles of shampoo, eighty-seven bars of soap.)

_____ yes    _____ no

Totals    _____ yes    _____ no

## Scoring

Count every yes answer as one point.

| | |
|---|---|
| 0-2 | Excellent. With your ability to cut out the clutter, it shouldn't take you very long to completely eliminate it. |
| 3-4 | Better than average, but there's definitely room for improvement. |
| 5-7 | Room for concern (and nothing else). Better not wait to begin eliminating clutter. |
| 8-10 | Fire hazard. Get out of the house, quick! |

Over the years I have heard (and admittedly, used) every excuse in the book for holding on to clutter.

I am convinced that there are about three people in the country who have come to terms with their own lame excuses for saving clutter and who have kicked the clutter-collecting habit. I am one of them. I think the other two are nuns. The rest of you are still clutterbugs.

The thing is, unused possessions are *useless*. That's why they are unused. As if being useless isn't bad enough, these pests have to cause all sorts of problems at your expense. They squeeze you out of your own home. They trip you and fall on you. You wind up climbing over and around them and for what? Not one good reason! On top of that you have to dust them, move them and insure them. They cost you money, inconvenience and peace of mind.

*Everyone* has clutter (except me and those two nuns) in one form or another. Clutter creeps into your life in a variety of ways. It comes as gifts, keepsakes, collectibles, decorations, investments, bargains, inheritances and hobby projects. In fact, it usually comes into our lives as a useful item. But, when an item has outlived its usefulness, it deserves a proper burial.

When it comes to housework, I am convinced that it's less the cleaning quotient than the clutter quotient that counts. It's the clutter that keeps you a slave! If you really understood how this stuff enslaves you, how much extra work and inconvenience it causes you, how much it costs you (monetarily and otherwise), you would surely move mountains to get rid of it.

But what if you are one of those people who has a difficult time letting go? Perhaps you hang on out of sentiment or frugality. Maybe you are convinced your pieces of junk are actually valuables in disguise.

Are these actually good reasons to hang onto unneeded and unused items? Check it out.

## THE PENNY PINCHING "SOMEDAY-ER"

Dan was like a man possessed. He loved shopping for bargains, he loved wheeling and dealing. He couldn't believe some of the stuff people practically *gave* away! They didn't even know what they had. "Why, with just a little work, this thing will be as good as new and I'll double my money!"

Yup, Dan loved every aspect of buying and selling. Well, not exactly *selling*. Oh, he had good intentions, but he was a busy man. These deals didn't just fall into his lap, after all; he had to go out and find them. That took time. Besides, running his own business kept him busy. Between work and scouting his deals, he barely had time for his family. But, he'd get around to fixing this stuff someday. Then he'd be able to sell it and make some money.

Well, old Dan sure did come across a lot of good deals. In fact, he did so well his garage was piled halfway to the ceiling with stuff. When he ran out of room in his garage, he just started piling the stuff outside. (This made him very popular with his neighbors.)

Dan had quite an enterprise going. The only thing was, he seemed to be getting deeper and deeper into debt. But, he couldn't let a little thing like that discourage him. "You have to spend money to make money" was his philosophy. He was a man of vision.

Dan became quite well-known around town. All the men in town always had a friendly smile and a wave for Dan. He made quite an impression on people. Not quite the impression he *thought* he was making, however. While Dan saw himself as a wise businessman, everybody else in town saw him as the biggest sucker west of the Mississippi. If anyone ever had any junk to get rid of, Dan was the man to call. He never did disappoint them either.

If you were to ask Dan's wife what she thought of all his wheeling and dealing, she'd say she's put it behind her. She's put Dan behind her too. She finally realized he loved his junk more than her and she left him.

As for Dan, he knows that great people are often misunderstood.

If you hang onto things because you think that someday you will restore, work on, fix, repaint, mend, repair, modify, upgrade, enhance or otherwise improve them, then what are you waiting for?

Or, perhaps you hold on because you have spent money on the item and you aren't sure you've gotten your money's worth. Remember that what you paid for was the *use* that item afforded you. Once it has been used, it has fulfilled its duty. If it actually wears out or breaks, it is useless. Motivate yourself to let go of this worthless junk by asking yourself these questions:

### If I don't have time to do it now why do I think I will have time to do it someday?

Are you expecting to hire a maid, retire or quit work, so that you will have time for these projects?

### How much of my time does the everyday business of life take?

Do I really want to spend the time I have left being distracted by, scouting for or refurbishing junk? Think about it.

*Even though I spent money on this item, it is now broken.*

I will probably have to spend even more money to repair it. Is it worth the extra investment?

*Even if I can repair this myself, is it really worth my time?*

Time is a far more valuable commodity than money. After all, it's non-renewable.

## THE SENTIMENTAL SOFTY

Ask any of her friends and they would tell you that Sue was the sweetest person you could ever know. She had a heart as big as the whole outdoors.

When Sue was a baby, her aunt gave her a beautiful porcelain doll for her first birthday. It became a tradition and forty-two years later she still had every birthday doll her aunt had ever given her. She also had every valentine she had ever received (at last count there were almost six hundred), and wrapping paper and bows from every present she had ever received. She had saved every invitation ever extended to her and had pressed every flower ever given to her by a boy.

Sue's house was like a museum of her life. Every wonderful thing that she had ever received was carefully preserved.

Then, the unthinkable happened. While Sue was out of town for the weekend, there was a fire. The fire department responded quickly and they were able to save much of the house. Unfortunately, a great many of Sue's sentimental keepsakes were lost in the fire. She was devastated. Her whole life was destroyed in a matter of minutes. It's been three years and she still hasn't fully recovered.

Sentiment is a strong reason for keeping things. We all have milestones in our lives and keeping mementos from those times is a way of keeping those fond feelings close to our hearts. Here are some suggestions for letting go of sentimental clutter.

### Concentrate on the precious memory.

You don't need to keep the thing to keep the memory. Objects are just symbols, just reminders of a happy event. For instance, your wedding was precious, your marriage is even more so. You need not keep every leftover napkin, invitation, bag of rice or other souvenir as a memento. How could you ever forget your wedding day?

### Rather than keep the object, keep a small photograph as a reminder.

This helps preserve the sentiment without taking up a lot of space. I learned firsthand how helpful this is when I had my son. I wanted to hold onto every outfit and toy. They were all so precious. I knew I couldn't, so I made sure I had photos of everything as a reminder.

### Save a selection of items, rather than the whole collection.

For instance, if you want to save baby items belonging to your precious little angel, choose a few favorites. Save some things that represent a span of time. Perhaps his hospital band, a favorite blanket, his first birthday outfit or first real toy. All the pictures you take will help remind you of the other things you gave away.

## HOUSEWORK HATER

Pam hated housework. It wasn't so bad when she first got married, but somewhere along the line she had grown very weary of the whole thing. There just seemed to be no end to it. She couldn't understand it. It was only her and her husband. How could two people create so much work? She often wondered what it would be like if they had children. She cringed at the thought as she dusted the crystal stemware hanging from the slats in the oak sideboard. "Gee, this oak dries out fast," she thought. "Time to oil it again already. That means moving all this crystal, the copper coffee carafe (that needs polishing), the plants (that could use some water), the candles, books, pictures, and all these other odds and ends. What a hassle."

While Pam worked, she daydreamed about all the things she would like to do in life, once she got caught up with housework and found the time. She had a whole collection of classic novels, but no time to read them. She had always wanted to write, but who had time for that? Where did the time go anyway? Oh well, no more time for daydreaming, that's for sure. There were plenty of shelves and bric-a-brac to dust.

If cleaning your house takes so much time that you are unable to pursue other areas of interest, then admit it: Your profession is that of a maid. If your possessions and decorating style have enslaved you, help yourself find freedom by asking these thought-provoking questions:

*Just how important are all these nicknacks, bric-a-brac and other decorating accessories?*
Important enough for me to spend large amounts of time dusting and polishing?

*When I am laboriously oiling furniture, meticulously polishing silver serving dishes, carefully dusting nicknacks, what am I missing?*

*Do I show more concern for my house than for myself?*
Do I spend more time working to improve my house than I spend working to improve myself?

Eliminating unused and unnecessary possessions is one of the biggest steps you can take toward freeing yourself from slavery to housework.

## NO BUTS

*If you are a collector, I suggest you be a collector of knowledge.*
Collect information that will feed your brain, rather than things that will crowd your house and create unnecessary work for you.

*If you are a sentimental softy, keep sentiments in your heart where they are most meaningful.*
Don't mistake the symbol for the happiness itself.

*If you are a penny-pincher, take solace in the knowledge that some things that you can no longer use can be used by others.*
If you've outgrown your wardrobe, give it to someone else who can use it. Now you get double your money's worth!

## LETTING GO — ONCE AND FOR ALL

I know how difficult it is to let go. I've been there. I also know how *liberating* it is to let go. I'm there now. I was once a hopeless saver of everything from old clothes and unfinished needlework projects to bits of aluminum foil and empty mayo jars. Now I'm the world's champ at getting rid of possessions and decluttering. You know what? It feels great! Talk about freedom. Not allowing yourself to be enslaved by absolutely worthless objects and philosophies is one of the greatest assets a person can have. You can't imagine the difference this personal power makes in your life. You have to live it to understand and appreciate it.

What helped me was a realization of how much time and energy I was wasting on clutter. I didn't have the time to dust it, the space to store it, or the inclination to insure it, so I got rid of it. I took a very close look at the things around me and decided which things made my life better. Those I kept. Then I looked for all those things that robbed me of my time and energy but didn't give me anything in return. Those I threw out.

There were hundreds of things that I got rid of over the years. So much so that I completely changed the way I decorated, the way I shop, and the way I dress. Every day I keep on top of clutter. As something wears out or breaks, I toss it without a moment's hesitation. That's the key. Once you declutter your life, you have to keep on top of it because clutter creeps back daily. The good news is, once you experience the great feelings of freedom, it will be easy to let go.

## HOW TO DECLUTTER GENTLY

OK, I've convinced you to eliminate some excess. The question is, where do you begin? Well, if there is something that you have been meaning to get to (I know you have dozens of such projects), by all means do. Perhaps you've been meaning to go through your closet and give unused clothes to charity. Maybe you've been meaning to go down to the basement and tackle all those *National Geographics*. Whichever you choose, be sure it's something you feel confident about tackling. Don't begin with the sentimental items. Start with something you believe is reasonable to eliminate. Once you experience the exhilaration of letting go of these things, you can move on to tackle those items that may prove more difficult to eliminate. When your courage falters, use the box storage system.

## THE BOX STORAGE SYSTEM

The box storage system is a simple, yet effective tool that is used to conveniently store items that are not used on a daily basis. It consists only of shelves and cardboard boxes; there is nothing fancy about it and anyone can set one up.

The idea is to have an easily accessible location for all types of storable items. It can be located in any of a variety of areas: the garage, basement, attic, utility room, office, or sewing or guest room. You may choose to use wood shelves, metal shelves or particle board. You may even want to set it up in a closet. You have lots of leeway to make it work in your particular circumstances.

You will find that your box storage system gives a home to all sorts of things. Items to store include:

- Seasonal items
- Sentimental keepsakes
- Holiday decorations
- Old paperwork, cancelled checks
- Infrequently used appliances and gadgets

I've found this system to be an invaluable aid. It eliminates so many odds and ends from under beds, crowded closets, cupboards and drawers. It relieves pressure from the garage, hall closet and linen closet. By using the box storage system, you can store most items in one location. Everything you need is at your fingertips. No more searching for something, wondering where it could be. In addition, it provides security for those people who have a difficult time letting go. If you have qualms about eliminating something, you can store it here. Eventually, you may find the courage to let it go. At least once a year (when doing spring cleaning, for instance), go through your boxes and eliminate anything you no longer need.

This is how it works: Each box is labeled with a generic category. Titles such as "kitchen," "toys" and "seasonal clothing." There's no need to specifically list the contents of every box. That's too much work and doing so would defeat the ease of using the system. Besides, the contents will periodically change. All you need is a generic title. If you are looking for the egg cups you only use when you have overnight guests, you would know to look in the kitchen box. If your youngest child is ready for some toys that the older one has outgrown, you check the toy box. If you need your winter scarf, you would check the seasonal clothing box. It's all very simple and extremely easy to use, once you get it set up.

In addition, it's a logical place to store those items that you want to keep but almost never need. Items such as your marriage certificate, your high school diploma, your old tax returns, and any other sentimental belongings. There's no point crowding your home with these things. The box storage system is the sensible solution and you will be able to locate them immediately if you ever do need them.

The beauty of the box storage system is that it takes everything out of nooks and crannies and puts it all together in one easily accessible location. And, it really doesn't take up that much space, especially when you consider the convenience.

For help with ideas on things that could be stored in your box storage system, review the list below. Check off items you would like to store and add others you may think of on the lines provided.

- [ ] art supplies
- [ ] auto care items
- [ ] baby clothes
- [ ] books
- [ ] boots/galoshes
- [ ] camera equipment
- [ ] camping items
- [ ] canning supplies
- [ ] children's papers/art
- [ ] church info
- [ ] craft supplies
- [ ] extra first aid items
- [ ] extra kitchen items
- [ ] extra linens
- [ ] extra pantry items
- [ ] greeting cards/stationery
- [ ] high school yearbooks
- [ ] hobby items
- [ ] holiday decorations
- [ ] household tools
- [ ] loose photos/albums
- [ ] magazines
- [ ] maternity clothes
- [ ] old paperwork
- [ ] party supplies
- [ ] picnic basket/supplies
- [ ] pool supplies
- [ ] record albums/tapes
- [ ] reference materials
- [ ] seasonal clothing
- [ ] sentimental baby items
- [ ] sentimental items
- [ ] sewing items
- [ ] sheet music
- [ ] skates
- [ ] ski boots/gloves
- [ ] sports paraphernalia
- [ ] toys
- [ ] trophies/ribbons
- [ ] vacuum accessories
- [ ] volunteer work/club
- [ ] warranties/receipts
- [ ] winter hats/scarves
- [ ] wrapping paper, bows

*What else might you store?*

☐ _____    ☐ _____
☐ _____    ☐ _____
☐ _____    ☐ _____

As you can see from the list, your box storage system can be used to house many items that would otherwise be taking up space in your closets and cabinets.

## TIPS

• Look for an inconspicuous location close to the main living areas (where you spend most of your time) to set up your box storage system.

• Purchase new boxes rather than use old messy looking ones. They will give your system a clean, orderly appearance.

• Look in your yellow pages under "Boxes" for a manufacturer in your area. The boxes are not expensive and can be shipped directly to you if you cannot pick them up. The manufacturer will most likely require a minimum order (probably twenty-five). This will not be too many.

• Ask the manufacturer for their recommendation on how to set up the boxes. (They will be flat when they arrive.) You could use heavy-duty tape. This can be messy, so try to be neat so you won't be disappointed in the appearance. An alternative is to use hot glue. This works well, but hot glue is tricky. Be very careful and wear gloves or keep a bowl of cool water handy in case you get a burn.

• Boxes are available in a wide range of sizes. Avoid purchasing boxes that will hang over the shelves. This is an important consideration when you choose a shelving method. I recommend the boxes be a minimum of 16″ long and a maximum of 24″ long. They should be 10″ to 14″ in width and 8″ to 12″ in height. Currently I am using metal shelves that are 18″ deep and boxes that are 18″ long by 12″ high by 12″ wide.

• Store only one category of item per box. Mixing categories will only cause confusion and disarray. When labeling the box, you may not want to label it directly, as the contents may someday change. I've used sticky notes (although these tend to fall off in extreme weather) and I've also used 3″ × 5″ cards attached to the boxes with double-sided tape. This has a nice appearance, and I prefer it to labeling the boxes directly.

It's difficult to convey how strongly I feel about this system of storage. I've been using it for many years now and I can't imagine trying to keep things under control without it. It has made the business of housework considerably easier. I believe you will find it an invaluable aid, once you give it a try.

## THE CORNERSTONE OF ORGANIZATION — ORGANIZING BASICS

In the first chapter, I promised to give you some organizing tips. Since I wrote a whole book on getting one's home organized, *The Organization Map*, it will not be easy to condense this information into such a short space. I will, however, share with you some key points.

As I've said, one of the cornerstones in your foundation for mastering housework is good organization. This refers to the way you do things (your systems and routines) as well as the way you store things. Good spatial organization means having a place for everything. This is an extremely important step toward mastering housework. Without this cornerstone in place, you will be cleaning around, shuffling, and tripping over your stuff every time you try to clean. That drives you crazy and will only perpetuate feelings of slavery. Being a slave to the things that are supposed to make your life more convenient is intolerable.

Though many people think it is impossible to have a home for everything, I can tell you from my own experience that it is possible. Of course, you do yourself a major favor by letting go of broken, outgrown, outmoded and otherwise unused items. Obviously, when there are fewer things to house, it is easier to make a home for those remaining. In addition, the box storage system comes in handy for items that you just don't know what to do with.

Now, let's take a look at the three steps to follow when organizing spaces and creating homes for your belongings.

### Step one: designate the purpose of the space.

When organizing and finding a home for items, it's important to have a clear picture of what you want to house in a given space.

Therefore, you designate the tenants of the space. For instance, let's say you want to organize the closet in your entry hall. You should make a list of all the things that will logically make their home in that closet, as well as anything else you may choose. For example, items such as coats and hats, boots and umbrellas. By creating this list, you will not only have a picture of what will make its home in this space, you will also have a clear understanding of what should *not* make its home there. That brings us to the next step for organizing and creating a home for everything.

### Step two: eliminate.

The second step in this process is to eliminate any and all items that no longer meet the guidelines specified in the designated purposes list. For your typical entry closet this means eliminating the basketball, the tennis racquet, the gym bag, and all the other odds and ends that get tossed in. Eliminating also means getting rid of duplicate items and out of season items whenever possible. Those can be stored in your box storage system.

### Step three: contain.

The third step in this process is to contain the remaining items. This means using baskets, hooks and organizing aids to contain items within a specific space in the larger space. For instance, in our entry closet example you may want a basket to contain winter hats and another for gloves. You may want hooks for the coats, a dishpan for wet boots, and a wastebasket or umbrella stand for umbrellas. By carrying through with all three steps, you can reach maximum efficiency and also make it much easier to maintain organization in the area. If you leave out this essential third step, you haven't reached your goal of creating a home for everything. Consequently, items will have a tendency to float around in the space and it will quickly become disheveled. To help make sure everything gets back to its proper home, label baskets, shelves, the inside of cupboard doors and so forth. It really does help.

These are your three steps for organizing. Don't try to leave a home without them.

## GENERAL ORGANIZING TIPS

• Store anything that is not used at least once a week in your box storage system. This would include all those small kitchen appliances and gadgets that you use only for specialty meals.

• When storing, group things that are used together in the same location, even if that seems odd. For instance, when you eat dinner, you use napkins and flatware with your dishes. So, store these items together in the same cabinet and get everything you need at one time.

• Be a labeling nut. Once everything has a home, label it. Label the insides of cabinet doors, shelves, in drawers, closets, everything.

• Store things off the floor when possible. This will mean using shelves and baskets in closets and hanging organizational aids as opposed to floor versions. Keeping things up and off the floor makes cleaning easier to do and more likely to get done.

• If you really have a lot of possessions, you may want to use two box storage systems. One is for unused items such as old paperwork and keepsakes. The other unit can be for more frequently used items.

The clutter shuffle affects not only what we save and squirrel away, but also how we decorate our lives. "Undecorating" our home is an important way of de-cluttering—which is why I've devoted chapter seven to the subject.

*Chapter Seven*

# UNDECORATING

A few years ago my husband and I were selling our house. While we were at work, and unbeknownst to us, a real estate agent made arrangements to show it. We had no sooner arrived home from work when the realtor and prospective buyer arrived, surprising us. We chatted a moment and then they walked through. When they finished their tour, the buyer asked me, "Have you been cleaning all day?" I said, "No. In fact, I just got home from work." He looked surprised and said, "Your house is immaculate!" Needless to say, that made me feel wonderful.

Over the years I've gotten many compliments on the cleanliness and condition of my home. People have often asked me, "How do you do it?" Well, I'm going to tell you one of my biggest secrets. Are you ready? Here it is: I keep my house absolutely devoid of decorative clutter. That's all there is to it! If you're thinking there's got to be more to it than that, I can assure you, there isn't. In fact, there have been many times when I have received the same compliment even though I hadn't actually *cleaned* for quite some time.

My secret is not in the techniques I use to clean what I have. My secret is not having to clean what I don't have. Simple, isn't it? You see, I prefer not to clean a lot of things I don't need. The less there is to maintain, the less effort I put forth in housekeeping.

In chapter one I explained the four cornerstones to lay in order to master housework. This is the cornerstone of uncluttered living.

## TO ACCESSORIZE OR NOT TO ACCESSORIZE — THAT IS THE QUESTION

My first house was a great place and I received dozens of compliments on how nicely it was decorated. I even had people asking for the

name of my decorator! The problem was that I had unwittingly created massive amounts of work for myself. Though my original motivation was to make our house a comfortable home, what I had really
done was to make our home a slavedriver, and I was the slave!

That experience was a good one because it taught me a lot about
what not to do when decorating. In our next home, I took a completely different approach to decorating and it drastically reduced
the amount of time and effort I put forth in housecleaning. I have
no scientific data, but I don't think that it would be overestimating
to say I cut the time I spent on some housekeeping chores by 500
percent or more.

I sold off many decorative items and quite a bit of furniture too.
As it happened, not long after our move my husband decided to
make a career change and went back to school. This meant that
there was virtually no money for decorating our new house. I had to
piecemeal some things together, but it was still a very pretty look
without all the extras that had caused me so much work.

I still received compliments on my new house, and lots of questions about my decorator. What was different was the amount of
time required to keep things looking great. I had cut that drastically
by moving from a somewhat cluttered style of decorating with lots
of shelves, wall hangings and plants, to a minimalistic style. I even
got rid of end tables that had been nothing more than places to park
lamps and catch dust. Any piece of furniture that wasn't absolutely
necessary was cast out to make room for nothing. It was great.

I have to tell you that there was a time in my life when I never
would have believed I would prefer the simple, minimalist look. I
had always loved the country look. But, after freeing myself from so
much work and enjoying that extra time, I fell in love with the light
and airy look. I now adore a bare wall.

If you feel defeated by housework, take heart. While there will
always be cooking to do, clothes to wash and beds to make, some
tasks can be eliminated. An easy way to start easing your burden is
to eliminate much of the work associated with your furnishings. I'm
not suggesting that you live in a cold, barren house. I'm just advising
you to be very selective in the way you furnish and decorate. It can
make a tremendous difference in upkeep.

## UNDECORATING – STEP BY STEP

If you would like to enjoy the benefits of less cluttered decorating, you will probably need to do your revamping in stages. For most people it wouldn't be practical to just toss everything out and start over.

You should also keep in mind that when I refer to decorating, I am not just speaking of accessories. Many people over*furnish* as well.

Now, remember the organizing steps you learned about in chapter six? We'll apply these here, too. We'll also look at specific suggestions for undecorating slowly. But first, I want to give you some help identifying clutter.

## IDENTIFYING CLUTTER

In order to help you identify items that may actually be clutter, let me describe a few different types that I had listed in *The Organization Map*:

### Atmosphere clutter.

Atmosphere clutter consists of items that are used for decorative purposes. Included in this category would be such things as:

candlesticks
vases
figurines
plants
nicknacks
sculptures
coffee-table books
wall hangings
potpourri pots

Of course, everyone likes to have some decorative pieces, but if you get carried away, you'll wind up exhausted from the excess work they cause.

### Snob clutter.

Snob clutter consists of articles that are seldom if ever used, are usually expensive or showy, and are intended to impress. Included in this category would be such things as:

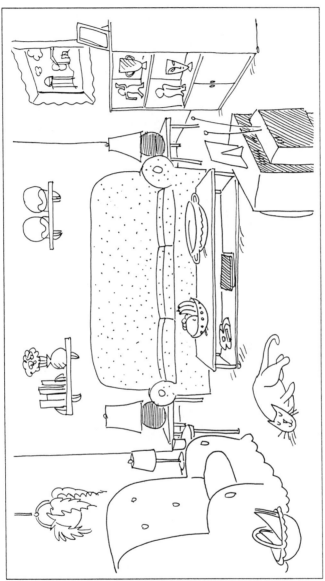

Here there are coffee and end tables cluttered with magazines, books, artwork, etc. The
walls are cluttered with shelves whose only purpose is to shelve more clutter. Every surface
is covered with nicknacks, figurines, candles, dishes, magazines, newspapers, books, vases,
etc. There is too much "visual clutter" on the walls and in general.

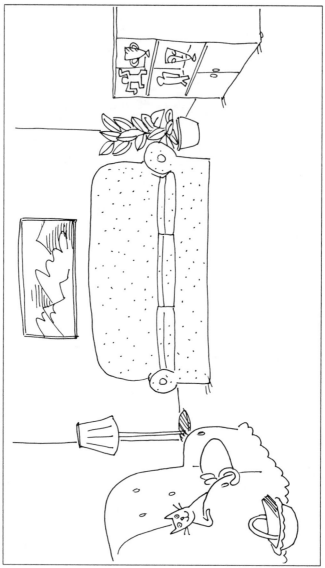

Here the tables have been removed. Their only purpose was to catch clutter and hold the lamps. A floor lamp replaces the table lamps. A lovely painting replaces the jumble of shelves, plaques, pictures, etc. A floor basket next to the chair catches the daily paper and a magazine or two. The figurines have been contained in one area — in the curio cabinet. This way they con't cause a cluttered look and they are also protected. The TV has been removed to the family room. There is now only one plant on the floor (in the corner).

crystal decanters
sterling silver tea sets
marble candy dishes
ornate carafes
gold-plated chess pieces

People line them up around the room and then neglect to use them.

### Masquerade clutter.

Masqueraders are perfectly useful items in good repair. The catch? They aren't getting used. Most families have several items that fall into this category. The children stop taking guitar lessons, yet there's the guitar in the corner of the living room. The puppy outgrew his doggy bed, but there it is by the fireplace. Dad quit smoking, but his pipe carousel is still on the table next to his favorite chair. All of this may seem painfully obvious now that I've pointed it out, yet it's easy to be blinded by the things we look at and take for granted every day.

### Someday clutter.

Someday clutter consists of items you hold onto, intending to get to, read, fix up or finish someday, as discussed in chapter six.

Stacks of newspapers
Piles of magazines
Half of an afghan you were knitting

Take a moment now to look around your living room (or whichever room you prefer) and on the list provided, jot down the things that could qualify as one of these four types of clutter. I'm not asking you to remove any of these items yet. I'd just like you to look through your living room with a critical eye, seeking potential offenders.

Atmosphere  _____

_____

Snobs  _____

_____

Masqueraders    _____

                _____

Somedayers      _____

                _____

Now that you have a list of potential clutter, what should you do next? Designate, Eliminate and Contain! As we did in chapter six. Review these steps so you know what you will be doing, once you actually begin to declutter.

### Step one: Designate.

To evaluate your furnishing needs for a particular room, you start by designating the purposes of that room. As an example, we will consider the living room. What types of activities take place in your living room? (If you also have a family room, you may be able to define the purposes very specifically. For instance, you may allow romping and television watching in the family room, but not in the living room.) Check off the appropriate activities below. Add any others on the lines provided.

- ☐ reading
- ☐ conversation
- ☐ watching television
- ☐ musical lesson
- ☐ playing, romping
- ☐ homework
- ☐ entertaining guests
- ☐ _____
- ☐ _____

Once you have done this, you have a guide. You have established the types of activities that take place in this room, and by omission, established those that don't. That automatically brings you to the next step.

### Step two: Eliminate.

Eliminate those things that no longer meet the designated purposes. In one seminar I taught, a woman confessed that there had been a broken stereo in her entry hall for fifteen years. I'm sure everyone in the family was so used to looking at it that it never crossed anyone's mind to get rid of it. It had become a fixture.

I grew up in a home with a baby grand piano in the living room. It might have been nice, if someone in the family had played the thing. As it was, it just took up a lot of space and collected a lot of dust (masquerade clutter). Look with a critical eye at the things you have in your living room and eliminate those items that don't meet any of your designated purposes or are not worth their keep.

### Step three: Contain.

As much as is feasible, contain items to one location. For instance, if you have a treasured collection of figurines, contain them all together in one display case. Not only will it help protect them from damage, it will cut down on your cleaning. Contain all your books in one room or group of shelves.

## DECLUTTERING TIPS STEP BY STEP

- Start with one room. Choose one in which you spend a lot of time. For instance, the living room.
- Get three boxes and mark each with one of these categories: Give away, Throw away and Sell.
- Begin with small items. Review the list of items you made in the section on identifying clutter. Work on eliminating small things from that list. Remove clutter from your walls, shelves, bookcases, tabletops and floor. If you have a terrible time letting go of things, ask yourself what's worth more to you, your furnishings or your time.
- As you collect items to discard, place them in the three boxes you have already prepared.
- If you are not quite ready to let go of something, yet are willing to try to eliminate it, store it in your box storage system. Perhaps once it is out of sight it will be out of mind and soon forgotten. Eventually you will have the courage to discard it entirely.
- If you simply can't let go of anything, then store some decorative items in your box storage system. In a few months, rotate those with the items still on display. At least by doing this you begin to get used to a less cluttered style and you may find you like it.

• If you have very large collections of things such as bookcases filled floor-to-ceiling with books, you may feel overwhelmed if you try to deal with the whole thing in one sitting. Pace yourself by dividing up the job. For instance, let's say you have a collection of five hundred books and are willing to let go of some of them. Plan to sort through two shelves or fifty books each time. Place those you intend to give away in a box and store it in your box storage system.

If you are afraid that having them so close will tempt you to retrieve some, then be sure to drop them off at the library or nursing home as soon as you have sorted them. Don't wait.

• Once you have eliminated some of the smaller items from the room, you can tackle the big stuff: the furniture. Go back to your designated purposes list and review the notes you made. Let's say you decide you are able to eliminate a table and a chair. The first thing you need to do is decide if you are going to give them away or sell them. If you decide to sell, place an ad in your newspaper right away. If you decide to give them away, perhaps to charity, either load them up or call the organization for a pickup right away. Get the items out of the house as soon as possible, so your courage doesn't falter.

## EVALUATING YOUR FURNITURE NEEDS

If you plan to be shopping for furniture anytime soon, why not make up a designated purposes list for the room you intend to furnish? This will help you evaluate your needs and determine exactly what you should, and shouldn't, buy. Most people actually need and use much less than they have.

## DECORATING DO'S AND DON'TS

Let's take a look at some decorating do's and don'ts for easy home maintenance. Bear in mind that you may occasionally come across some pieces of furniture or accessories that please you so much, you are willing to do the necessary upkeep. That's fine, as long as you know what you are in for.

### Walls

Rarely do you see a blank wall in someone's home. Because of their size and number, walls are almost always loaded up with decorations. The problem is that furnishing your walls doubles your work. If you want to create a look for your walls, consider such simple and elegant treatments as paint and wallpaper. These can decorate without requiring the upkeep associated with other things.

**Do's.** Paint. Use paint treatments to create a subtle or dramatic effect. For instance, a two-tone scheme: soft peach, accented by off-white on ceiling, door and baseboard moldings. A beautiful look on its own which, unlike wall art, requires no dusting or polishing.

Wallpaper. A variation on painting. There are many possibilities. You could try a wallpaper border near the ceiling or perhaps one pattern on the upper half of the wall with a complimentary pattern or even paint on the other half, divided by wainscotting.

Stenciling. A time-consuming but lovely alternative. Just don't overdo it or you will suffer from visual overkill. Stick to a below ceiling treatment with accents around door frames. Also, a light, sparse pattern is better at conveying the feeling of lightness than a heavily detailed or scrolled pattern. Easier to do too.

Any of these are nice on their own. You could add one painting or print, or perhaps a wreath and you are done! Truly, a beautiful painting or print is nicer to look at and easier to maintain than a dozen odds and ends.

**Don'ts.** Don't use dark colors when painting or papering, unless you specifically want to create a dramatic look. Dark colors not only add a feeling of heaviness, they also tend to visually constrict a space, making it appear smaller.

Don't use shelves on your walls as a means to house nicknacks. For easy maintenance, shelves are better used for books. Empty shelf space is only an invitation to place a statue, vase, candle, or some other dust collector.

Don't cover a wall with two dozen pictures, plaques, needleworks, and other odds and ends if you can use one or two larger pieces. Doing so will cut your work dramatically and make the room more attractive.

## Lamps

Whenever possible, choose floor lamps over table lamps. This eliminates the need for tables and their resultant upkeep. Choose a sleek design. Avoid heavily pleated shades or fabric shades with bows and flounces.

## Tables

What purpose will these serve? Do you really need them? If you decide to go with end tables, look for a design with an enclosed cabinet. This will allow storage and keep odds and ends from piling up on or under the table. Avoid mixing mediums such as wood and glass. Two different surfaces require two different cleaning methods.

## Bookshelves

Having to make storage for a lot of books you are unlikely to reread is silly. If you insist on keeping them, store them on bookshelves (preferably an enclosed cabinet, to cut down on dust) and avoid placing any nicknacks amongst them on the shelves. This will make dusting easier and less time-consuming. If you decide to give them away, a local library, charity, nursing home or community center may be interested.

## A FINAL WORD – DECORATING WARNING

If you flip through the pages of a home decorating magazine, you are likely to get a headache from some of the design combinations. With eighteen different patterns on walls, drapes, chairs, pillows, carpets and couches, I literally get dizzy just browsing. Add to that the enormous amount of accessories added to give a lived-in look, and you're ready to jump through your skin.

Pay no attention to interior designers and their nutty ideas. I can't believe some of the ridiculous suggestions they come up with while unsuspecting clients sit there nodding, thinking their designer must be very chic. Recently I saw one boasting about some old suitcases she had stacked on top of each other to make an end table. (Rather tatty looking, not to mention precarious.) Later she showed a wall display of antique farm tools. Hmmm, dusty, rusty, *attractive*. If you want low maintenance, pay no attention to these ideas.

*Chapter Eight*

# AN OUNCE OF
# PREVENTION

W ell, so far you've learned how to schedule your chores to get routine tasks accomplished regularly, how to include family members in the housework, how to decorate for minimum maintenance, and how to sort through and store clutter. If you have employed these techniques, your life should already be easier.

Of course, you must be wondering if you can *prevent* the dirt in the first place. The answer is no. The truth is, there isn't much we can do about dust and dirt. Since we can't eliminate them, we can't eliminate our work. However, there are a few things we can do to curb their entrance into our homes and reduce our work load. I'll share some general ideas for preventative measures you can take.

In addition to dealing with dirt, our work includes keeping general order in the home. One of the most frustrating parts about cleaning is all the preliminary work that needs to be done. Quite often people spend as much time picking up and putting away as they do cleaning tasks. Consequently, maintaining orderliness is another important facet of prevention. So this chapter contains tips for mess prevention in specific rooms of the home.

Let's first explore some of the larger concepts related to reducing work, then look at specific things to do in each room.

## GENERAL DIRT-CURBING CONCEPTS
### Inside/Outside Door Mats

This is an idea I got from cleaning expert Don Aslett. Don believes that a large portion of the dirt that gets into our homes is tracked in on shoes and boots. We wind up expending a lot of energy, time and even money trying to get rid of this dirt. Of course, any sensible person would do everything they could to reduce it coming into their home in the first place, right? Well, you've got two choices to overcome this problem.

You could do as the Japanese do and request that everyone remove their footwear at the door. This may work for some families who could use a basket with slippers nearby to help the transition. However, cold weather will present problems, and of course, many people would feel uncomfortable asking visitors to remove their shoes. So, if you can't get the shoes off the people, then you will have to get the dirt off the shoes.

You've probably noticed that the floor in your entry area looks worse than the floors in other areas of the house. That's because it collects most of the gunk from your shoes. If it's wood or linoleum, small rocks and pebbles caught in soles can pit and scratch it. Carpeting isn't any better; it just gets stained.

The solution then, is to have mats that catch the majority of the dirt before it makes itself at home in your carpet and flooring. Not just any old mat will do either. I'm sure we've all had bad experiences (not to mention death-defying falls) on those little throw rugs and carpet samples usually used as welcome mats. (Welcome to the emergency room is more like it.) What you want are mats that will *stay* in place. That means they will remain where you put them and not slide and creep their way into the neighbor's yard or wander through the house. The surface must also be porous enough that it will rub the soles of the shoe and scrape off the dirt.

The ideal type of mat for this purpose is available at your local janitorial supply. They are rubber-backed, nylon mats that come in just about any color and size. If possible, try to get one long enough to accommodate four strides of the longest-legged person in the house. Most of the grit should be knocked off by then.

Popularly used in commercial businesses, these mats can help at home as well. Though they are not exactly cheap they are not inordinately expensive either. When you consider the work and headaches they reduce, they are a bargain. They may be vacuumed, or hosed down and hung to dry. Put them at front and back entrances as well as at the garage entry. Invest your money in these helpful aids and you will save your time and energy.

## Air Duct Cleaning

Anyone looking at a sunbeam streaming through their windows on a sunny afternoon has noticed the whirl of dust particles. It's disconcerting to see so many things swirling around in the air that we breathe. Unfortunately those same particles are there even when the sunbeam is gone. Since air quality affects our lives, comfort levels, and even the amount of dust circulating, it makes sense to keep the air in our homes as clean as possible.

A relatively new service available is that of air duct cleaning. Companies specializing in this service are able to seal off your air ducts and do an air wash (forcing air through the system at high pressure and then out into a vacuum). This process dislodges accumulations of dust, animal hair and mold that has built up over the years. Once done, you shouldn't need the service again for five to ten years.

Used with proper filtering, this helps keep the air in your home cleaner and circulates less debris. Many claim that not only does it keep the house cleaner, it helps allergy sufferers as well.

Unfortunately, even the professionals disagree about the proper type of air filter to use. Some claim the newer electrostatic filters are a modern marvel, while others prefer the older models. Whichever style you choose, either replace it or clean it frequently for maximum benefit.

## Food

The more casual you are about where your family eats, the more trouble you will have cleaning. Spills happen. When they happen on carpet, the results can be disastrous. Not only is it a bother cleaning the spill, there's always the chance that a permanent stain will result.

To free yourself from unnecessary slavery to spills, stains, crumbs and vacuuming, limit eating to the kitchen and dining room. If your dining room is carpeted, you may want to consider having a wood floor installed instead. Be sure to have it sealed with polyurethane. The only real cost is monetary since it will actually save you a lot of aggravation.

### Below Ground Rooms

If part of your living space is in a basement area, you have probably noticed more dust there than in other parts of the house. When we lived in a tri-level home, the lower level was partially below ground. That portion of the house was always much dustier than other areas and it drove me crazy. I finally figured out that I had to keep the windows down there closed because there was just too much stuff making its way through the screens. I decided to get my fresh air from upstairs windows. It made a big difference.

### Animals

As much as we love them, animals are a big source of dirt and work in the house. If you don't mind the work associated, they can be great companions. However, if you are looking for every conceivable way to lessen your work load, avoid furry pets. The two most common house pets, dogs and cats, are like people in that they track the outdoors in. Dirt, mud and bugs can all enter the home via their paws. On top of that are the hairy coats. Not only do they shed, they also manage to pick up twigs, leaves and burrs and carry them in like luggage. If you want to keep Rover and Muffy, then at least do the following:

- Use the mats suggested previously.
- Bathe or groom them frequently.
- Restrict their access in the home. Some people help curb the work by training animals to stay out of certain rooms of the house.
- Keep them off the furniture. If keeping them out of certain rooms seems too harsh, then at the very least keep them off the furniture. Dirty paws on the floors and carpets are bad enough, but hair and dirt on the furniture is really unnecessary.

### Newspapers

If you are in the habit of reading the paper in your favorite lounge chair or spreading it across the floor as you watch your football games, be aware of the ink that it leaves behind. Who hasn't read the newspaper only to have to go wash their blackened hands when they are finished? The ink that makes itself a nuisance on your hands also makes itself at home on your furniture and carpets.

I'm not suggesting that you give up your local news, but you should dispose of the paper as soon as possible. Leaving it to lie around will not only cause clutter, but may stain something as well. If you insist on keeping it, have a magazine rack or basket to hold it.

## MESS PREVENTION AND ORGANIZING TIPS ROOM BY ROOM

### Kitchen

- Let every family member have their own special mug or tumbler that they use throughout the day. It can be hung on a mug rack or returned to a special shelf. This prevents them from grabbing a new one each time they drink. A large family can easily go through two dozen glasses in a day.
- If you have a commercial-style water dispenser, keep little paper cups nearby, as well as a trash basket. They can get a drink and toss the cup without leaving a mess.
- To curb unexpected kitchen cleanups, "close" the kitchen between meal times. This prevents the problem of sandwich fixings all over the counter at 3:00 in the afternoon.
- Hang a special bulletin board for art projects, instead of using the refrigerator door.
- Have a special place for lunch boxes so they don't get left out on the counter every night.
- Keep an office-style message pad by the phone so messages can be accurately taken. Have a message bulletin board nearby so that everyone can get their own messages. If feasible, mount it on the inside of a cabinet door. This reduces visual clutter.
- While chatting on the phone, organize a cabinet, clean out odds and ends from the fridge, or clean out the junk drawer. Just don't make too much noise or your friend may think you rude.
- Keep snacks in a specially designated cupboard or drawer so family members don't have to rifle through every one searching for something to eat.
- Rather than line spices up along the top of the stove back,

keep them in a basket on a cupboard shelf. The basket is easily grabbed in one motion and you won't have such a mess to clean off the stove.

- When working with doughs or meatloaf, use slick butcher paper or even a paper grocery bag to protect the counter. When you are finished, the whole mess gets thrown away and you still have a clean counter.
- Also when working with sticky foods, keep a wet washcloth close and wipe fingers before opening drawers or cabinets.
- Do not add any kind of open shelves to the kitchen, either for storage or decorative purposes. This is the opposite of prevention.
- Soak pots and utensils in sudsy warm water while you eat, and cleanup will be easier after dinner.
- If you have a little hand vacuum in the kitchen, one of the kids will probably get a kick out of sucking up the crumbs on the floor. Doing this will prevent them tracking around the rest of the house.
- If you have a closet in the kitchen, you may want to put a full-size rectangular garbage can in it. Use the kind that allows one side of the lid to stay attached at all times. Insert a plastic garbage bag and use for trash. It takes longer to fill than kitchen size wastebaskets and all you do is remove the plastic bag and take it outside.
- Line trash containers with several plastic bags. When a full bag is removed, a new bag is already in place.
- Pull the plug on buffet-style eating, which only means food spills and trampling feet throughout the house. Kitchen and dining tables were made for such prevention and convenience.
- When mopping your floor, keep your bucket stationed in a corner or up against a wall or cabinet. This will help prevent accidental spills where you don't want them.
- Always keep a working fire extinguisher close at hand.

## Living Room

- Keep a large wicker basket in a corner for stray toys to be tossed into.

- Keep a special basket, tray or folder near your easy chair for school papers you need to look over or sign. Let your children know to deposit them there, so they won't get scattered. If you prefer, this could be kept in the kitchen.
- To prevent stains and crumbs, do not allow snacking in the living room.
- To prevent accidental drink spills, have children drink from a sports cup or some other type of cup with a lid and tiny hole or straw to sip from.
- Do not allow briefcases, school books and coats to lay idle on tables and chairs. Designate specific homes for them in the entry closet or the owner's bedroom.
- Cancel subscriptions to magazines that go unread. Keep only the current issue of magazines. Have a designated magazine rack in which to keep them stored. Keep only today's newspaper.
- After dinner, or about an hour before bedtime, have someone go through the room with a laundry basket, picking up stray items. These can be carried to the owner's room and deposited there.

## Bathroom

- Keep counters absolutely clear.
- If you have no drawer space, you could use baskets as drawers. House categories of items together: hairbrushes and combs, makeup, shaving gear, toothbrushes and toothpaste. Keep them in the cabinet or closet.
- If you have drawers, use drawer dividers and small baskets to create a place for everything. Label them. It's more fun for kids to put things away if they have an easily identifiable home.
- Use a shower caddy in the stall to keep shampoos, conditioners and soaps from floating around. Also, limit brands of shampoo. Forty-two bottles are forty-one too many.
- Have enough towel holders so that everyone can have one for their own personal towel which can be reused throughout the week. If you need to add more, do it. You could use the circular style which doesn't take up too much space. Or, use the bar

style and hang a couple on the back of the door, one high and one in the middle of the door.

- Have men prevent a furry sink by putting down paper towels before trimming their beards or mustaches.
- If there is room, keep a laundry basket in the bathroom (preferably in a closet) so that dirty items don't get left on the floor.
- Keep glass cleaner and a cloth nearby (away from children) and do a quick wipe down of the mirror, sink and chrome when you are finished washing.
- Do not use shower doors and save yourself oodles of work.
- Keep a sponge or even a squeegee hanging in the shower stall. Toward the end of your shower, wipe down tile or walls while the water is still running. Gets rid of shampoo, conditioner, soap splatters, and makes weekly cleaning easier.

## Kids' Rooms

- Have routine toy cleanup times. For instance, before lunch, before dinner, and a half hour before bed.
- For easier cleaning, avoid fish, frogs, turtles, gerbils and birds.
- Limit toys. Have a policy that a few old ones must leave if new ones are to be brought in.
- Use a few laundry baskets as hampers. Line the bottom of the closet and let them sort clothes into cleaning categories as they undress. If possible, color code the baskets. Whites such as socks, underwear and T-shirts go into the white basket. Jeans and other darks into the dark blue basket. Brightly colored T-shirts and so forth into the red basket.
- Designate one drawer in the dresser for "worn once but OK to wear again" outfits. Otherwise they will be hesitant to put them away with the clean clothes and they'll get left on the floor or piled on a chair.
- Have a specific hook or drawer for pajamas that can be worn again.
- Mount coat racks or hooks for hats and jackets.
- Give children a file box and files for paperwork and art.
- Avoid dust ruffles and avoid some of the dust. Use a comforter alone, instead. It won't drag on the floor and collect gunk.

## Office

**Preventing paper.** Paperwork piles are an aggravation as well as a mess. Help yourself deal with paper more effectively by implementing the following suggestions.

- Have a mail-processing system for paperwork. Use either hanging files or paperwork trays for each category and immediately sort mail into these when it arrives. This technique helps you make sense out of something that is often overwhelming and stems the messy tide of incoming paper. It only takes a few minutes.

To do: Things to take action on.
To file: Things to file when you have the time.
Spouse: Mail for your spouse.
Financial: Bills to be paid.
Mail: A holding tank when you don't have time to separate. It's better than leaving it out where it is bound to wander.

- Have a large wastebasket at your desk and immediately throw away junk mail. Don't even open it, it may be too tempting for you.
- Set a specific time each week to pay bills and keep up with paperwork.
- Don't hang onto materials that you don't have time to read this week, thinking you will have time someday.
- If you have lots of informative pamphlets, magazines and brochures, pull out only the pages with articles you want to read. The rest can be tossed out.
- If you or your spouse has a briefcase crammed full of paperwork, organize the papers into the same categories as above, using folders.
- If you receive lots of catalogs and enjoy browsing through them, you may want to create an additional tray or file like those mentioned above for the catalogs. At least they will be contained in one place, rather than floating around.

**Designate — eliminate — contain.** When looking for preventive measures to keep a house clean, help yourself find solutions by using my three-step method.

Designate the problem.
Eliminate the dirt when possible.
Contain the dirt if you can't eliminate it entirely.

The three-step process of designate, eliminate and contain is a major concept for me. I have been able to apply it to many facets of organizing and cleaning. I have also found that it can be useful when trying to figure if or how you can prevent cleaning woes in the first place. When faced with a cleaning problem, reason it out in this manner.

**Designate the specific problem.** What is the problem you are facing? For instance, the entry hall floor is always dirty because people track in dirt on their shoes.

**Eliminate the dirt.** Since dirt in the hall is your problem, you must prevent it from coming in. How can you do that? Ask everyone to remove their shoes? Perhaps there's a way to get the dirt off the shoes before they come into the house. This could be accomplished by having heavy-duty mats at the entry areas which will knock most of the dirt off the shoes before they get inside the house.

**Contain the dirt.** Keep the dirt from spreading throughout the house by requiring that people remove their shoes in the house. The shoes can be kept in a basket, dishpan or some other container that will trap the dirt.

This three-step thought process may not work for every dilemma, but it may prove helpful in finding answers to many of them.

*Chapter Nine*

# THE SOLUTION?
# FIX THE PROBLEM.

## THE PROBLEM

T he best part of any problem-solving expedition is, of course, the solution. Solutions to housekeeping problems are easier to come by than you may think. The main obstacle to overcome is your own complacency. I have found both personally and professionally that most of us quickly get used to inconveniences. We may moan and groan about them, but we learn to live with them. This is a big mistake. By accepting these frustrations, we wind up living with an undercurrent of aggravation that eats away at our well-being. Not only does it make housework less tolerable, it gives us the feeling that we don't have control over our workplace.

Even when the inconveniences are relatively minor, a continual battle in our workplaces or our own homes eats away at our peace of mind. Taking the time to find and implement a solution to these problems is worth the effort.

The thing is, you will remain a slave if you battle with a problem over and over again simply because you haven't taken the time to find a solution. Though you may not be able to solve every housekeeping dilemma, you can certainly do something about most of them.

## THE SOLUTION

The most important part of finding the solution to a problem is to recognize and clearly define the problem. This may seem incredibly obvious, but complacency often renders us blind. Have you ever had the experience of visiting someone's home and noticing how much trouble they go through to do the simplest task? Maybe they have to squish between an old chair and table in the entryway to get to the closet. Maybe they have to take out half the pots in the cabinet to get to the one they want. Perhaps they have to position the faucet just right so it doesn't leak or bang twice on the side of the refrigerator to make the buzzing noise go away. Chances are, if you pointed this out to them they would laugh and say they hadn't even noticed. They are so used to those things. *Recognizing* and *clearly defining* the problem are the first steps.

Next you should diagnose what is causing the problem. Sometimes this is relatively easy, sometimes it's not. Using an example above, the person who has difficulty getting to their closet should reason in this manner: "I am having trouble getting to the closet to hang my coat. What is causing the trouble? The table and chair are in the way. Why are the table and chair here? Do they serve a useful function here? Are they as important as the closet?" If they are not of equal or greater importance than the closet, the answer is easy: Remove the table and chair.

For some of you, this may seem ludicrous. You may be thinking "Do people really have these problems?" I can assure you, they do. It's not that the people involved are not intelligent. It's just that they have grown so accustomed to dealing with these daily inconveniences they really don't even notice them anymore. (Perhaps yours aren't so obvious, but I'd wager you have one or two yourself.)

The next step is to think of the most logical action to take as a result of your discovery. I have to thank my husband for pointing this out to me. Several years ago he saw me battling with something and suggested, "When something isn't going as smoothly as you think it could, stop and figure out what hinders your progress and then think of what you could do to fix the problem." I myself was so used to putting up with things, it took my husband to point out the obvious. Fortunately, my creative mind has helped me to come up with solutions to problems that arise around the house. In years past, I bemoaned such problems and demanded: "Why doesn't someone come up with a solution to this?" Now I come up with the solutions myself.

So, I encourage you to look anew at the follies and foibles that fill your daily life. There are probably dozens of things that you have learned to live with.

Following are some common household problems with suggestions on actions you could take. These may solve some of your existing problems, but they also serve as examples of how to identify a problem and come up with a logical solution.

## 1. The Problem

When family members arrive home they dump their books, pocket change and briefcases on the kitchen counter. They are left until Mom does something about it.

### *The result.*

This is the sort of thing that drives Mom crazy. Not only does it make an unsightly mess, it gets in the way. The kitchen counters get enough of a workout from meal preparation. On top of that, Mom feels that her family has no respect for her. She feels like a maid.

### *The solution.*

Figure out why your family members are not putting their personal belongings away when they come home from school and work. Are they merely inconsiderate? Do they need a reminder from you? Perhaps they don't know where to put these odds and ends. Is there a specific home for these items?

- Make it so easy for them that they can't avoid cooperating. If you have already tried asking everyone to put their belongings away when they get home and that hasn't worked, try thinking of another solution. Set up a storage system for every item at the entry that is most often used by family members.
- Hang baskets with compartments, labeling each with individual's names. Use these for depositing pocket items.
- Set up a small bookshelf for book bags and briefcases.
- Put up a wall-mounted coat rack for jackets and use a large basket for shoes.

By having a specific place for each of their items they can deposit all those things in their homes before they even enter the house.

## 2. The Problem

After dinner everyone makes a beeline for the TV and Mom is left to clean up by herself.

### The result.

Mom starts drinking.

### The solution.

Nobody is helping and it takes Mom a very long time to clean up on her own. She misses out on time with her family and feels worn out and frazzled. She knows that if everyone would pitch in, the job would get done quickly. What can she do?

- A new rule is implemented. Before anyone is allowed to watch TV they each must remove their own place setting, rinse it, and put it into the dishwasher.
- Each person must then return to the table to take one or two items back to the kitchen to be put away. This could even be broken into categories.
- One person takes the condiments back and returns them to their proper places.
- Another person takes the leftover food, puts it in refrigerator containers, and then puts it away.
- Another person removes the place mats and tablecloth and stores them.

This method works well for a large family because the whole job is completed in no time.

## 3. The Problem

Your three active sons are constantly running in and out of the house and tracking dirt and mud all over the place.

### The result.

Mom starts seeing a psychiatrist.

### The solution.

First, figure out why they are running in and out. (There is probably some method to their madness.) Are they constantly going to their rooms for the baseball, bat, and other sports equipment and toys? Talk to them about which toys they usually play with outside.

There's really no reason that the bat and ball should be in their bedroom.

- Outdoor equipment can be kept in an outdoor shed, toy closet, or even a large plastic garbage can. As long as the lid stays on the can, the toys should be protected from rain.
- If the reason they keep coming in is to get something to drink, install a drinking fountain faucet on your outdoor spigot.
- As for curbing the mud, take cleaning expert Don Aslett's advice. Go to the local janitorial supply and purchase the indoor/outdoor mats that will catch much of dirt before it gets into the house. (See chapter seven.)

## 4. The Problem

In your two-story house, people are always taking things downstairs but they never return them to the upper floor.

### The result.

Ninety-nine percent of what you own is in the living room.

### The solution.

Put a large basket close to the stairs. (Not so close that people can trip over it.) Instruct your family to drop their personal things in the basket. Make it an assigned job that someone carries the basket upstairs at bedtime (or whenever) and drops things off in the owners' rooms. This system will probably work better if this job is rotated on a weekly basis. Those tempted to fill up the basket for an unsuspecting sibling will have to face the music the next week themselves.

## 5. The Problem

Family members are snacking on key ingredients for recipes.

### The result.

Everyone is getting sick of having omelettes for dinner.

### The solution.

Have a way of designating which items can be eaten and which need to be saved as a dinner ingredient.

- Set aside a shelf in the pantry for "do not eat" items. Family members will know that this area is for items used in dinner recipes that week and will snack on something else.
- If your space is very limited, you could use a coding method instead. For instance, use a permanent marker to make a big black "X" on packages that are to be left untouched. Another idea is to use little colored stickers. Use a specific color as a warning to leave this item alone.
- Another solution is to have a snack drawer or shelf. When family members want a quick bite between meals, they know they can safely grab something from this special place without ruining dinner plans.

## 6. The Problem
Your family members keep coming to you at the last minute every morning and asking if you can sew a seam or take up a hem.

### The result.
Mornings are very hectic and you think you are getting ulcers.

### The solution.

- Teach everyone in the house how to sew.
- Institute some type of mending schedule. Set up a mending box near your sewing machine and instruct everyone to put items that need mending there. (You should have them mark the spot that needs mending with a safety pin so you won't have to search.) Explain that mending will be done once a week on such and such a day and if an item is not in the box, it will have to wait until the following week to be mended. Tell them to check their clothes the night before because you don't intend to do last-minute sewing. This may seem harsh, but it's only sensible. Mornings are hectic enough.

## 7. The Problem
Your children forget to clean out their lunch boxes when they come home.

*The result.*

You find UFO's (Unidentifiable Food Objects).

This is especially terrifying on Monday mornings.

*The solution.*

Remind them to do this chore by linking it to another part of their routine. For instance, if they usually have an afternoon snack, they should clean out their lunch boxes before they eat. If they don't snack, use something else as a reminder: before they watch TV or take a music lesson. Of course, another alternative is to use paper bags, which are disposable.

## 8. The Problem

Your husband leaves his socks on the floor.

*The result.*

You invest heavily in air fresheners.

*The solution.*

Assuming that requests have gone unanswered and even nagging hasn't worked, you've really only got a few more choices. Of course, you could simply put them in the laundry basket yourself, remembering how much you love him. Or, you could just leave them where he drops them. He should notice them piling up after a few days. If he doesn't notice the piles, he will eventually notice the empty sock drawer. Explain your new policy: If it's not in the laundry basket, it doesn't get washed.

## 9. The Problem

Though they have all been told, your family members still neglect to check their pockets before dropping items into the hampers.

*The result.*

Dad is not thrilled about wearing pink undershorts.

*The solution.*

Give them a reason to remember. Tell everyone that they need to be checking their pockets. Let them know that from now on, any items you find in their pockets will go to "jail." This can be a box, basket or other container that you use to house these objects. The owner will have to pay you "bail" in order to get the item out. The bail amount is set by you. It could be a chore or even a small cash fee. You want it to pinch enough that they will be more thoughtful next time they put something in the dirty clothes. On the other hand, you obviously can't charge more than the item is worth because they will have no motivation to get it out. If you just wind up throwing away a lot of gum wrappers, call your charge a sanitation fee.

## 10. The Problem
The whole family vies for time in the bathroom every morning. This always escalates into an argument.

### The result.
People are clean or stinky on alternating days.

### The solution.
In a case where a whole family shares a bathroom, careful scheduling is an absolute necessity. You should list the times that each person needs to leave the house. There will probably be some variance. If everyone leaves together, it will be tougher.

- Make a schedule that allows the first person who leaves the house the privilege of being the first to use the bathroom. Continue in this manner, allowing those who leave at earlier times to use it before those who leave later.
- Give each person a maximum of fifteen minutes in the bathroom. Install a wall clock so they can be aware of the time. If that doesn't work, use an egg timer.
- Make sure everyone has a mirror set up in their rooms so grooming and makeup can be done there, leaving the bathroom free for others.

I hope these suggestions will help with some of your problems. As you face others, remember to be very specific about identifying the problem. Decide on your ideal outcome, what you want, and then on a logical scheme to solve the problem. It's a little like a detective solving a mystery, and it can actually be fun, especially when the problem really *is* solved.

*Chapter Ten*

# WORK SMART NOT HARD

W ell, we had to get around to it sometime, the actual cleaning process. We may as well just face it and get it over with.

I am not a professional cleaner. I am a homemaker and an organizer. I am not qualified to write a book on "101 Nifty Ways to Use Muffin Mix and Palm Fronds to Clean Your House." I'm just a regular person who has a regular way of cleaning.

I have, however, been the proud recipient of scores of compliments regarding the cleanliness of my house. Since I take a certain amount of pride in cleaning as *infrequently* as possible (two times a week and sometimes only once), I figure I must be doing something right.

By now my methods should be clear: The most effective kind of cleaning is the kind you *don't* have to do.

I'm convinced that it's less the *cleaning* than the *clutter* quotient. In an uncluttered room, a television set with an inch of dust on top will be less noticed than a spotless, dust-free room that is rife with toys, magazines, newspapers, nicknacks and other paraphernalia. Remember this: A crowded room, no matter how clean, seems less clean than a slightly dirty but uncluttered room. If you have taken that concept to heart, than you have probably already removed much of the clutter in your home (chapter seven) and done what you could to prevent the dirt in the first place (chapter eight). If not, then you will have to be prepared to do the necessary work and keep the complaints to a minimum. If you believe these items are important enough to own, then they are important enough to maintain properly.

## Doing Your Own Thing

I consider housecleaning to be a personal thing. Each one of us needs to go about the process in the easiest, most comfortable way. Consequently, I don't intend to lay down any hard-and-fast rules or insist that you adhere to them. I simply want to present some information and let you decide which bits and pieces make sense to you.

Over the years, I've read lots of advice from cleaning experts and while I respect their experience and opinions, I don't necessarily take their advice. I think the suggestions they make often work better in a professional cleaning situation, rather than for a homemaker cleaning her own home. When you are cleaning your own place, you have a vested interest. I believe it's completely different than a person who does this as a job. They have to have a system for getting through a house, but that doesn't necessarily mean their system will feel comfortable to you.

So, don't be intimidated by experts who tell you there is only one way to clean. Though they may have excellent advice, it won't do you a bit of good if you don't feel comfortable with the routine and consequently don't do it. The best advice in the world is useless if it's not applied.

Before I give you pointers on the actual cleaning process, let's look at some basic information to prepare ourselves for the job.

## Your Cleaners

To peek into the cleaning closets in some homes, you would think there must be surgery taking place on the premises.

Cleaning supplies are a personal thing. I've heard people rave about products I really don't care for at all. How can you decide which to use?

Well, first of all, continue to purchase commercial household products at the grocery store, experimenting with brands until you find those you prefer. Or, buy your supplies at the janitorial supply company in your area. Some of the cleaners are concentrated and need to be diluted according to the directions. Others come ready to use in smaller containers.

One thing I *don't* recommend is that you concoct your own cleaners. Not only can this be deadly, it just doesn't make much sense.

You can buy them at a reasonable price, already mixed and packaged. Your time is of great value and saving $.23 by mixing your own window cleaner just isn't worth the bother.

Now then, how many cleaners do you need?

### Kitchens and bathrooms.

For cleaning these rooms, you want a *disinfectant* cleaner. You probably hear a lot about these on commercials, but do you know what they do? Disinfectants are agents that actually inhibit the growth of microorganisms, tiny living organisms, sometimes parasites, that can have a pathogenic (disease-producing) quality. Yum. Just what you want as a side to that meatloaf.

### General cleaning.

For this type of cleaning, you can use a neutral cleaner, neither acid nor alkaline. It can be used for everything from mopping your linoleum to cleaning the drip pans on your stove. It is not a disinfectant, so use it where bacteria are not of concern.

### Multipurpose glass cleaner.

Use this for cleaning glass, mirrors, chrome and appliances.

The nice thing about these cleaners is that they clean a wide variety of things and you needn't stuff your closet with cleaners for each individual task.

Those are your actual cleaning products. You'll need a few other supplies from that same janitorial supply company.

## CLEANING SUPPLIES

### Plastic spray bottles.

These are inexpensive and you need them if you will be mixing the cleaners with water. Be sure to clearly label the bottles with a permanent marker.

### Lambswool duster.

Don't you hate pushing dust around, only to have half of it wind up in your eyes and nose? Lambswool works well for picking up rather than pushing around dust. If you purchase the style with the long handle, you may be able to reach high spots without a step stool. When using a duster, be sure not to slap it around. This allows the dust you have already captured to be let loose. If you need to release some dust, tap it on your shoe so that the dust will fall to the floor where it can be vacuumed.

### Ostrich-feathers duster.

An alternative to the lambswool duster, made from the black feathers of the male ostrich. I have had bad experiences with feather dusters, but these have a natural oil that seems to attract dust.

### Treated dusting cloths.

Yet another alternative to those already listed, these are chemically treated to attract dust. They come in a package of six and can be thrown away when used up.

### Terry cloth cleaning cloths.

I sometimes pick up inexpensive terry facecloths and use them too. You can pop them into the washer for cleaning. (A damp cloth is great for dusting washable, non-wood items around the house.)

I consider these the basics. Depending on how far you want to take this, you may also be interested in:

a squeegee for your windows
extension handles that allow you to dust in high places
pumice stones (to remove toilet bowl rings)
professional floor waxes
gum freeze (an aerosol you can spray on gum to make it hard so it can be removed more easily)
enzyme digester (for urine and vomit)
scrubbing pads
sponges
dust mops
cleaning cloths
floor squeegees (similar to for window squeegees, but used for floors)

I caution you to keep your wits about you when you visit the janitorial supply store or you may wind up with nifty supplies and cleaners that you don't really need.

## OTHER TOOLS

I'm always amazed at some of the cleaning equipment I see people struggling with. A vacuum that exhales more than it inhales is not a friend. Having the proper tools to do a job is essential. Any job, even a relatively easy one, can be rendered impossible if tackled without the proper tools. Good quality cleaning supplies and tools are long-lasting and will save you time.

Here are some tools:

### Vacuum.

If you consider this a tool for sucking lint out of your carpet, then an upright vacuum is probably all you need. Personally, I find canister vacuums so unwieldy and uncomfortable that I have never purchased one. Some people like them because they come with attachments for cleaning upholstery and drapes, but uprights are now available with these features.

I use an upright vacuum with the biggest motor available. It also has edge cleaners and a handle that tilts down low for reaching under tables and chairs. A rubber bumper helps avoid gouging fragile furniture. If you hate switching plugs all the time, invest in a heavy-duty extension cord and leave it with the vacuum.

### Cleaning caddy.

It's convenient to use a tray to house spray bottles, cleaning cloths, a feather duster and other supplies. Beware of leaving it in low places if you have a youngster about.

### Kangaroo pouch.

A utility apron with pockets for keeping stuff at your fingertips. Personally, I don't like the bulk associated with this. Besides, with my method of cleaning (see page 112) I don't really need to have everything quite that close at hand. However, by carrying everything with you, you save a few steps and can clean whatever is in front of you at the moment. This works well for the person who cleans a whole room before moving on to the next. Aprons are available commercially, or you could make your own. If you make one, use a sturdy fabric such as canvas.

### Storing Cleaners

If you have small children in your home, I suggest you keep all your cleaners together in one location. Store them in a high cabinet where they will be out of sight. It's far better to walk a few extra steps to get your cleaner than to have the constant threat of danger because cleaners are stored under sinks and in other easy-to-reach locations. I keep all my cleaners together in my laundry room.

Another benefit of keeping them in one location is that you know what you do and do not have.

It's also wise for grandparents visited by small children to follow this advice. It's easy to forget about the dangers posed to little ones, especially if you haven't had to worry about this problem with your own children for many years.

If you have no children in your home and are never visited by people with small children, you may prefer to keep cleaners in the specific location where they are used. If you do this, I recommend you have enough for each area. In other words, if you have more than one bathroom, have duplicate supplies so each room can store what is needed.

As much as possible, keep all cleaning supplies with the cleaners. Store mops, brooms, buckets and cleaning cloths in the same location so you only need to make one trip.

Now that you've got your cleansers and supplies stored, let's move on to the actual cleaning process. There are two basic methods: item cleaning and room cleaning.

## ITEM CLEANING VS. ROOM CLEANING

The room cleaning method entails working your way through a room in a clockwise fashion, cleaning whatever is in front of you. This means doing all the types of cleaning as they are necessary: dusting, polishing, cleaning mirrors, vacuuming and mopping. You would clean the entire room before moving on to the next. If this is how you like to clean, use an apron to keep your supplies close at hand.

The item cleaning method means cleaning all the similar items at the same time. For instance, if you are in the mirror-cleaning mode, you would clean all the mirrors in the house, or the section of the house that you are working on. If you are vacuuming, you vacuum all the rooms moving from one to the next without stopping to do other types of cleaning in between.

I've tried both and prefer the item cleaning method. Actually, I combine the room and item cleaning methods. When I'm cleaning, I want to clean the entire room, but I don't like to move through it constantly switching from dusting to polishing to cleaning mirrors. Rather than move around the room clockwise, cleaning whatever is in front of me, I clean all the items in a category before I move on to the next cleaning procedure. I dust everything that needs to be dusted, and then I move on to polish everything that needs to be polished.

This seems logical to me and I think it makes the cleaning flow easier than the constant switching modes of the room cleaning method. In the end, it doesn't matter *how* you clean just as long as you *do* it. You should do what works best for you.

## FIRST THINGS FIRST — HAVE YOUR PLAN

So, to master housecleaning, you should do the following:

### 1. *Know when you will be cleaning.*
Create a simple schedule and then follow it.

### 2. *Know what you will be cleaning.*
This is part of your schedule. Choose specific days to do specific jobs. By doing this you will be less likely to amble around the house wondering what to do next.

### 3. *Do your preliminary pickup.*
Before you dive into cleaning, make sure everything is out of your way so you can get the job done quickly. That means going from room to room, straightening and putting things away. If you don't do this first, you will be forever starting and stopping.

### 4. *Gather your supplies.*
If you have decided to use a carry tray or an apron, load them with your necessary supplies: your liquid cleaner, cleaning cloths,

duster, polish or oil, and polish cloth. A couple of additional items you may find helpful are a scraper, an old toothbrush and a whisk broom. The scraper (a windshield scraper or a metal spatula) will remove odd lumps of unidentifiable origins. The toothbrush helps dust and clean in tiny cracks and crevices. A whisk broom is handy for getting the dust that gathers in corners that the vacuum can't reach. It also helps fluff sections of matted carpet before you vacuum. Of course, both of these jobs can be done with your full-size broom as well.

### 5. Make double use of time.

Don't wait until your bathroom is scrubbed and all the floors are mopped to start the laundry. Start a load first, then begin the cleaning. If you are planning to clean the oven (and it's not self-cleaning), spray the cleaner and allow it time to work while you wash the dishes. Whenever possible, allow cleaning solutions or appliances to be working at one job while you tackle another.

### 6. Work with gravity.

There's no point working *against* it; you'll never win. Whenever you are cleaning, start from the top and work your way down. This means if you intend to dust the entire den, first hit the cobwebs in the ceiling corners, then move to the curtain valances or door and window frames. Follow those by dusting shelves and picture frames. You want to work your way down so that dust doesn't wind up back in a location you have already dusted. Dust everything else before you dust and polish the end tables or vacuum the carpet.

This is exactly how I clean my house.

• On Mondays and Thursdays I do my heavy cleaning. I start by putting a load of laundry in the washing machine. I do whites first, as they require hot water.

• Next, I do general pickup. If you have quite a few things that need to be put away, grab a laundry basket and go through the areas you intend to clean. Place items needing to be put away in the basket. If you like, you could deal with each basket before you begin your cleaning. If you feel that is too much of a distraction, you may want to do it after the cleaning has been completed.

- Next, I dust. This doesn't take an inordinate amount of my time because as I've said, I have few nicknacks. I work with gravity, starting in high locations and working my way down. I go through the entire house and dust floor to ceiling.
- Next, I polish. Actually, I use oil on my wood furniture. I do it the same way as I dust, top to bottom. I don't polish *every* time I clean. I have always used Old English Lemon Oil. They also make a good spray version.
- After I polish, I clean mirrors. Again, I go through the entire house cleaning mirrors. For this job I use terry cloth washcloths. (I don't clean bathroom mirrors until after I have scrubbed the bathrooms.)
- After I have cleaned the mirrors, I sweep the kitchen and bathroom. I sweep the crumbs out of the rooms and onto the adjoining carpets. I use a broom with angled bristles. At this time I vacuum only the areas where I have swept crumbs onto carpets, near the kitchen and bathrooms.
- Next I scrub the bathroom (a more detailed description follows). Then I mop and rinse all the floors.
- Next, I vacuum every room. Currently I am using the Eureka Boss, because it had the biggest motor available at the time I purchased it.
- During all this I have loaded and unloaded clothes in the washer and dryer. Anything coming out of the dryer gets hung up (some things will later be ironed) or folded and put away immediately. I do a maximum of three loads.
- Lastly I iron.

On paper it doesn't look that bad, but it is a lot of work. I choose to get it all done this way. Someone else may prefer to do dusting and polishing one day, mopping another, laundry another. As I said, it doesn't matter how you do it, as long as you do it.

## IF IT AIN'T BROKE DON'T FIX IT— THINGS YOU CAN IGNORE

I chose Mondays and Thursdays as my cleaning days because I wanted the house to be in tip-top shape at the start of the week as well as on the weekend. However, Thursday's cleaning is a much lighter version of Monday's. I still do the basic routine, but I don't have to look for ceiling cobwebs, polish the furniture or mop the floors. I gladly skip anything that really does not need to be done again so soon. If the tub looks okay, I leave it; if the mirrors are spot free, I move on. If a room doesn't need vacuuming, I skip it. It's my choice to exercise mastery over these routine tasks. If I did more than I actually needed to, I would be a slave.

- Regularly polishing silverware that is only brought out at holidays. (Just polish it when you use it.)
- Washing the measuring cup you used to measure water.
- Ironing both towels and sheets.
- Meticulously folding underwear before putting it in a drawer.

As well as things like:

- Cleaning and recleaning the kitchen because you allow a continuous stream of "snackers." ("Close" the kitchen between meals if necessary.)
- Spending inordinate amounts of time ironing clothes that were forgotten in the dryer. (Just retumble with a wet towel and some of the wrinkles should come out.)

If you have that much time on your hands, you're definitely doing something wrong.

## BATHROOMS AND KITCHENS

Housecleaning is essentially a generic term for a variety of different tasks. The two areas of the house that actually require the most *cleaning* are, of course, the kitchen and bathroom.

Keeping the kitchen clean is important because this is where meal preparation takes place. There's no point in being choosy about fancy cuts of meat, only to leave them sitting unwrapped on a counter cleaned with the same sponge you just used to wipe the floor.

Similarly, the bathroom is a resort for germs. Humidity, moisture and bacteria are all commonplace in this tiny space. The dichotomy is that this is where people go to get *clean*. When they wash off all their personal germs, some get left behind. A clean, pleasant bathroom is important. It's really not too hard to get, if you do it properly. Here's advice for keeping up with both.

## Cleaning the Bathroom

First of all, the bathroom is not the place to display your gift for decorating. You've got plenty of other rooms in the house in which to bewitch and beguile your family and friends. Concentrate on function, ease of cleaning and timeliness of upkeep here. In an average-sized, uncluttered bathroom, you should be able to do a thorough cleaning in ten minutes. I do.

For my weekly deep clean, this is what I do: First, I spray the tub and shower stall with cleaner and let that start to work. Then I go to the sink and wet it, sprinkle a little cleaner (Comet), wipe the counters off, then wash the bowl. I do all of this before I clean the mirror so it doesn't matter if it gets spattered. Once the vanity and mirror have been cleaned, I do the faucet. I spray the faucet with the liquid cleaner, which does an excellent job of removing water spots. Not very often, but once in a while, I will use an old toothbrush to get into the crevices and hard-to-clean spots.

At this point, I return to the tub and wipe it down. I do not use shower doors as I consider them a cleaning nightmare. Lastly I turn to the toilet. I work my way down. I wipe the tank top and tank. (I don't use toilet covers.) Then I clean the bowl and lastly the base. By the way, I've read horror stories about women using bleach or mixing cleaning chemicals to deal with stubborn rings in the toilet, and then passing out. Never mix cleaners! If you have a ring problem, try using a pumice stone on it.

The last step is to mop the floor. I use the item method on that, mopping all the floors in the house at once. It just seems easier to me to get the bucket and mop out once and have at it.

For quick daily cleaning, I wash the sink of toothpaste globs, wipe the chrome faucet, and then wipe the mirror. If the room is still moist from the running shower, I don't even use a glass cleaner. This all takes less then two minutes and leaves the bathroom with that freshly scrubbed look.

## Keeping Up in the Kitchen

Cleaning the kitchen can be a real bugaboo. Besides the once a week floor mopping, there's daily cleaning. And it's not even once a day: it's breakfast, lunch and dinner, plus snacks, coffee breaks and homework marathons. Unlike other areas of the house that are cleaned once or twice a week, the kitchen is constantly being cleaned. At least, parts of it are. Here are some tips for making it easier.

## Preventing the Messes

One of my general rules for organization is: The greater the number of people who use a space, the fewer the items that should inhabit that space. That means a big family should have a bare kitchen. Get rid of the clutter. The kitchen really needs to be *clean*. The easiest way to keep an area clean is to limit the number of items in that area.

So, do yourself a favor and free up that much needed counter space. Get rid of (or store in cabinets or the box storage system) anything that you don't use at least two or three times a week. If your canisters are more decorative than useful, can them. If you rarely use the blender, get it off the counter. I learned to be ruthless when I was a newlywed and had a small kitchen. I ran right out and bought all sorts of helpful (I thought) kitchen gadgets and appliances and lined them up around the counters. I quickly learned what a pain it was to move sixteen things to wipe the counter of bread crumbs (which sprout wings and fly at the tiniest waft of air current). It also meant that there were sixteen more things that needed to have that sticky, fuzzy kitchen grease regularly cleaned off.

This concept goes for decorative items too. Everyone wants their kitchen to be homey and inviting, but if it's unnecessarily difficult to clean, you won't do it as often as you should. A kitchen with pretty but fuzzy, greasy, dusty decorations will *not* be homey. Exert your decorating energy in easy care ways; use washable vinyl wallpaper or borders to brighten and decorate. Use easy-to-wipe, clean, semigloss paints for adding colors to walls. With so much going on in the kitchen, it really doesn't require a lot of decorating anyway.

## Whistle While You Work and Clean Up As You Cook

Your whole house is in motion, but the kitchen is really the place where you exert your energy and thinking skills. It seems to be in a continual state of flux. First you are doing and then you are undoing. You put the clean dishes in the cabinet and then a few hours later take them out and dirty them up. You put the food in the refrigerator, then you take it out and pound, knead, chop and otherwise maim it all over the countertops. You clean the stove top of the lunchtime soup spills and shortly bubble and splat the night's spaghetti sauce all over it again. Like the hamster on the wheel, around and around you go.

Well, unless you plan to stop eating or hire a cook, you will be dealing with these problems for a long time. Invest a little time in planning and you can save time and aggravation in the long run. Here are a few simple but effective tips.

• When preparing food *always* put some soap and water in the sink. As you mix and measure, slip bowls and utensils in the warm water to soak. Before you grab for another stirrer, dip the one you have in your hand, then rinse it and reuse. Now you just have one to wash instead of two.

• Keep a damp sponge on the counter next to the stove. Use it to wipe spills and splatters right away.

• Do your unpackaging, your peeling, and your skin and fat trimming near the garbage. If this isn't feasible, hang a plastic bag from a nearby chair or drawer pull. Or, stand a paper grocery sack on the counter next to you. This will prevent you carrying (and dripping) garbage across the kitchen.

• When assembling recipes, line up all needed ingredients. If that's not feasible, line up the category of ingredients, for instance, all dry ingredients. As soon as that stage is complete, put them away in their proper homes. You have everything you need as you need it, but immediately have your counters clear again for the next stage. This also helps keep drawer and cabinet doors a little cleaner since you are not constantly reaching for things with meatloaf on your fingertips.

• Make a conscious effort to use fewer mixing bowls and utensils. Rinse and reuse these you have already worked with, rather than grab a clean bowl.

• If you are going to be making a mess, such as baking bread or making pies, use some type of wrapping paper to cover the counters. This can be balled up and tossed, leaving the counters much cleaner.

## A Few Odds and Ends

• If you don't have soffits over your kitchen cabinets (if the area above the cabinet is open to the ceiling), you could try this trick for keeping them dirt- and dust-free. (I learned what a pain this look was in my first home. At first I thought it was beautiful.) Anyway, I purchased inexpensive dishtowels and laid them on top of the cabinets. This caught most of the dust and grease. Periodically I tossed them into the laundry for washing. An alternative is to use something like newspapers, wax paper or aluminum foil to lay on top of the cabinets. Either can be balled up, thrown away and replaced. Do this regularly. Just be sure there are no light fixtures or other sources of heat close to the paper or fabric.

• Use nonstick drip pans on your stove. These are more expensive than the metal style, but are a big savings in time and aggravation.

• For a pleasant atmosphere while cooking or cleaning, you could keep a radio in the kitchen. Pretty music or an interesting talk show can keep your mind occupied and seems to make the time pass easier. Another nice touch is to simmer something that smells good. I and my family like cinnamon or cloves. Cheap, but a really homey touch.

• Use a catch-all basket instead of a junk drawer. I use this method and it really has cut down on the problem. (Junk drawers tend to multiply.) Any odd item (your neighbor's puppy's chew toy, an extra combination lock, your granddaughter's mitten) can be tossed in here until you are ready to deal with or return it. The rule is you may never get a second basket, and you must deal with each item once the basket is full.

• If you have messy recipes in your meal plan (fried foods, spaghetti sauce) put a easy-to-wipe backsplash behind your stove. It should cover the whole area between the stove top and the fan above. It's a snap to wipe with a sponge and saves paint and wallpaper.

## Chapter Eleven

# QUICK CLEANUPS AND SPEEDY SPIFFUPS

S everal years ago I realized that I had some specific housekeeping pet peeves. Though some chores weren't so bad, a few seemed unbearable and truly made me feel like a slave.

One of these heinous jobs was that of unloading the dishwasher. What an aggravation! What a waste of time! That I should have to slave away for hours to do this tedious task was simply intolerable.

Naturally, I would put off doing it for hours, even days. Sometimes I never actually got around to unloading. As a result, the dishwasher often served more as a cabinet. Whenever I needed a clean dish, fork or pot, I'd just open it up and grab what I needed. Using this peculiar method, it would eventually be unloaded in a couple of days.

One day I decided to time myself and see just how much of my precious time this miserable task took — without hurrying it took me two minutes. Perhaps you can guess that I felt pretty silly. Here I had wasted hours of my time agonizing over this little task when simply getting it done was much easier. Since that time I have never given a second thought to unloading the dishwasher. Oh, it still doesn't thrill me, but at least now I know that I will only have to endure it for two minutes.

Many people actually spend much more time dreading a job than they do completing it. Often, this is because they have a misguided notion that a job will take too long to perform. Housecleaning encompasses dozens of jobs. Many of these can be successfully completed in spare moments here and there. In this chapter I'll offer a host of ideas for chores that can be done in two minutes or less, five minutes or less, and ten minutes or less.

As you are improving your housekeeping skills, keep tabs on how long it takes you to get jobs finished. By being aware of the time you are spending, you may be able to find ways to improve on your time and spend even less on the task.

Besides being helpful information for you, knowing approximately how long a particular job will take is useful information when asking family members for help. If they moan and groan you can confidently reply, "This will only take five minutes."

## QUICK CLEANUPS

Little jobs like these can make a big difference in the appearance of your home as well as its function. It makes good sense to use small bits of time productively and every chore you finish now is one less to do later.

### Things That Can Be Done in Two Minutes or Less

Unload the dishwasher
Wipe down kitchen counters
Wipe drip pans on stove
Clean the faucet chrome and the mirror in the bathroom
Wipe up small spills in the refrigerator
Wipe down washer and dryer
Clean the lint filter on the dryer
Clean the inside of the microwave
Wipe down the toaster or coffeepot
Sew a button
Change a roll of toilet paper
Wipe switch plates in the kitchen
Dust the mantle
Reshelve books
Put stray magazines back in rack
Dust television and clean screen
Shake out a small doormat
Disinfect all the doorknobs in one room

### Five Minutes or Less

Dust one room
Sort mail into mail handling system
Take out the garbage

Scrub kitchen sink well
Clean out odds and ends from the refrigerator
Make your bed
Combine like condiments
Clear off message board
Wipe fingerprints from kitchen cabinets with soapy water
Set the table
Fill the salt and pepper shakers
Straighten utensil drawer
Rinse out school lunch boxes
Spray air freshener throughout the house
Fold a load of laundry
Make a to do list
Balance your checkbook
Hand wash several pairs of nylons or kneehighs
Write a thank-you note
Change kitty litter
Wash out the dog's food dish and give him fresh water
Check all your cleaning and laundry supplies, list those needed
Empty ice cube trays into bowl, refill trays, and put all back into freezer
Check the batteries in your smoke alarms and replace if necessary
Wipe crumbs and spills from the oven
Put away all your VCR tapes or compact discs
Dust the stereo
Sweep the hearth

## Ten Minutes or Less

Sort through a junk drawer
Scrub toilet, tub and sink in one bathroom
Clean all the mirrors in the house
Vacuum one room
Polish the coffee and end tables in the living room
Reorganize one kitchen cabinet
Dust the windowsills in all the bedrooms
Sort the laundry
Load the dishwasher

Check and change light bulbs throughout house
Vacuum under couch cushions
Iron a shirt
Shine a pair of shoes
Sweep the service porch
Water plants
Clean out your handbag
Hand wash a blouse
Roll up some pennies from your change jar
Put newly developed photos into album
Straighten jewelry drawer
Sew a patch
Fill potpourri dishes throughout house
Pretreat stains for laundry
Make a shopping list
Clear kitchen cabinets of seldom used appliances and store in your
    box storage system
Group all the clothes in your closet by category—dresses, skirts,
    shirts, etc.

## SPEEDY SPIFFUPS—QUICK ANSWERS TO SPECIFIC CLEANING PROBLEMS

No matter how well intentioned we are, no matter how carefully we plan, disasters sometimes happen. The Christmas cranberries wind up on the oriental carpet. The dog has an accident. The lasagna erupts all over the inside of the microwave. Well, here are some answers to the problems we all face now and then. They are grouped by category so that you can find them in a hurry.

### In the Kitchen

First, use discretion when purchasing appliances. Avoid anything black, great for a police investigation (shows every fingerprint) but lousy for a family. Next, do purchase the textured finished refrigerators. This makes loads of difference and I anxiously await the textured version of ovens, dishwashers and toasters.

*Q. How can I clean dried-up pancake batter from the stove top?*

You can't, so just buy a new one. Just kidding. Actually, the best thing to do is saturate the batter with an all-purpose cleaner, or if you don't have any, use plain warm water. Let it soak in. Using a soft sponge, remove what you can. If necessary, repeat the technique. Let the liquid do the work. Never use a powdered abrasive or steel wool. Now, get in the habit of keeping a damp sponge on the counter as you cook so you can swipe these messes before they adhere.

**Q. How can I keep the burner pans on my stove presentable? Should I wrap them in aluminum foil?**

No! Aluminum foil can catch fire. Make frequent use of the aforementioned sponge. For dried-on stuff, soak the rings and pans in hot soapy water. Do this as often as necessary until you remove most of the grime. Soapy steel wool pads work well if you have to scrub. They will probably scratch, however. Do yourself a favor and get the Teflon-coated style.

**Q. I've noticed an unpleasant smell from my wood cutting board. What can I do?**

Get rid of it. Honestly. Wood boards not only absorb odors, they are breeding grounds for bacteria. Every time you trim your meat or chop your vegetables, you leave behind new little cuts in the wood. Meat juices and food particles get in and the resulting bacteria sit around waiting to pounce when you slice your cheese or cut up your carrots. The proper upkeep is simply too laborious. Switch to a plastic board which you can wash in soapy water after each use. Always clean the board between categories of food. For instance, don't use the board to cut meat, then immediately cut vegetables.

**Q. Speaking of odors, my garbage disposal has halitosis.**

If it is otherwise working properly, the odor probably stems from bits of food that are getting left behind. Be sure you run it long enough to grind up everything, and keep that water flowing so that it will all be flushed away. A temporary help is to put orange peels in and grind away. They leave a pleasant citrus odor.

**Q. I love my microwave, but how can I keep it clean?**

Basically by using the same principle you use with the stove top and counters. Get to the spills quickly. However, in the event that you get distracted for a day or two, here's what to do. Create some steam by putting a cup or bowl of water in and heating it. The steam will help soften the blobs. Also, when cooking something messy (sauces) or explosive (potatoes, hot dogs) try cooking in shorter bursts of time and checking on the progress.

## In the Bathroom

*Q. I seem to be forever battling mold on my shower curtains. Any advice?*

Yes, excess moisture causes mildew and you can't get away from moisture in the bathroom. Run the fan while showering and even after to aid in drying things. After the shower, draw the curtain across the rod so that it is spread open and will be easier to dry. (Keeping it bunched up at one end of the rod keeps it wet.) Be sure your rod is hung high enough that the curtain doesn't stand in soapy water. Rather than fight the mildew when it does eventually win, use inexpensive liners behind your curtain and replace as often as necessary.

*Q. I can't keep my shower doors clean enough. What works?*

A shower curtain. Seriously, consider removing those pesky things. I hated them when I had them. They really serve no useful purpose and are a pain to clean. If you can't bring yourself to rip them out, hang an inexpensive liner behind them, just as you would with a fancy shower curtain. In the meantime, to remove that white haze, I found Lime-Away helpful, but you really need to use it regularly. You could find a more potent strength of cleaner at your janitorial supply.

*Q. Do those toilet tank drop-ins really do any good?*

I believe they do! I've heard some so-called experts say they do next to nothing, but that hasn't been my experience. I use the dissolving clear version. It has a bleach that really does help keep the bowl cleaner between washings. You may even be able to reduce the frequency of scrubbings if you use this product.

One negative I have heard is that the bleach is too harsh on the fixture. I've never known any homemakers who have complained about this, but personally I'd rather have a plumber replace my toilets every twenty years (if necessary) than scrub more often than is absolutely necessary. Toilets can be replaced; you can't.

**Q. My commode cover and bath rug always seem matted and worn looking. Is there anything that will help?**

Yes, a proper burial. Like so many others, I fell for these warm and cozy little rugs for the toilet. They look cute, pretty up the room, and give a sense of warmth. For about a minute. Then they start slipping around because they never quite fit. The elastic wears out and they just hang, misshapen. They catch every speck of lint from snapping towels, dots of flying toothpaste and shaving cream. Face it, they are more trouble than they are worth. Since they serve no real purpose other than decoration, they are not worth the upkeep. If you decide you love extra work, keep them and wash and dry them regularly. Replace them when they begin to get bedraggled.

**Q. Although I scrub my bathroom once a week, I still notice an unpleasant odor between cleanings.**

This is almost certainly from the toilet area. Check the seals on your toilet to be sure that there isn't any leakage. If not, it could be that someone is missing the boat, so to speak. Between regular scrubbings, lift the seat and spray the rim with a disinfectant. Also hit the floor around the base and the bottom of the base itself. Let it stand a few moments and then wipe. Try this one time between cleanings and see if you notice an improvement.

**Q. We just bought an older home and the toilet has a terrible ring.**

You probably live in an area with hard water. The ring is a buildup of mineral deposits. Since the previous owners didn't know how to remove it, you're probably stuck with several years buildup. You need to be able to get at it with a phosphoric acid cleaner, but you have to get the water out of your way first.

This can be accomplished by flushing the toilet and turning the knob on the wall behind the base when the water is drained from the bowl. This temporarily turns off the water, allowing the cleaner a chance to work. Apply your cleaner and let it soak before you scrub.

## Carpets

*Q. My little boy wants a puppy. I hate to deny him, but I dread the messes.*

Before choosing a breed, speak to your veterinarian about those with temperaments that blend well with children and are quick learners. As soon as possible, take the dog to obedience training. One way to curb the messes is to limit the animal's access through the house. In other words, the linoleum in the kitchen is easier to clean than the plush carpet in the living room. By limiting its access you can limit potential problems. I know people who have used this technique with great success.

*Q. Is there any surefire way to eliminate stains from the carpet?*

Unfortunately, stains are just that, stains. A stain actually dyes the color of the carpet. A spot on the other hand, may be removed. The key, of course, is quick action. For that you need to be like a Boy Scout, always prepared.

The problem is, I have encountered disagreement between carpet manufacturers and professional carpet cleaners regarding the best substances to use. While some carpet manufacturers recommend a 3 percent solution of hydrogen peroxide to aid in removing beet and grape juice stains, the carpet cleaners cringe at the thought. Their concern is that you are just as likely to take the color right out of the fibers in the carpet.

Another problem I have encountered is that some manufacturers are still recommending dry cleaning solvent to remove certain types of greasy stains even though it's virtually impossible to find. It's unlikely that you'll be able to purchase it from a dry cleaner or a carpet cleaner. The Environmental Protection Agency has too many restrictions regulating its use.

Besides, it's just too dangerous and it can damage the backing of the carpet if used improperly.

So, what should you do? If you know the manufacturer of your carpet you could call their customer service number and request information on treating spots. Presumably they will give you the latest information on treatments they have discovered. Your local carpet dealer can probably give you their number. If not, call 800 number information at (800) 555-1212. The manufacturer should be able to send you pamphlets that will describe how to deal with a wide variety of spills.

Another thing to do is to shop around for a respected carpet cleaning company in your area. Ask around until you find one and call them to see if they have a spot kit that they sell. Since it's not practical for them to come to your house for one spot, some cleaners have developed spot treatment kits to sell to their customers.

Of course, the best defense is a good offense. Have rules against eating or drinking on carpet. Refuse to allow anyone to eat their jelly sandwich or drink their grape juice in rooms with carpeting. I learned the hard way, but this really is the best way to handle the problem.

Of course, the unexpected happens. Without warning a child is sick, a guest spills coffee or a pen leaks. So even if you are careful, you may want to be prepared with a stainbusters kit. Keep your supplies in a carry-style tray, ready to grab. Store it in a safe place. Here's what to include:

- Plenty of white absorbent cloths. These could be terry washcloths or even cloth diapers.
- Liquid dishwashing detergent. I've used Dawn for years and like it very much. Diluted with water it gets out many stains. Mix one quarter teaspoon with one quart of water. Always rinse with clear water to remove traces of detergent. This treatment works for red clay soil, top soil, blood, beer, colas, jelly, eggs, milk and orange juice.
- Enzyme digester — these products are usually available at pet stores (some veterinarians or animal hospitals might sell them). Used for stains such as milk, vomit, blood and pet urine.

- Isopropyl rubbing alcohol — can be used in place of dry cleaning solvent on things like grease, oil, lipstick, crayon, spaghetti sauce and ink.
- Vinegar — Mix ⅓ cup white vinegar with ⅔ cup water. Can be used on beer, coffee, teas, wine and perfume.

### Spot removal steps:

- Before you treat a spot, test your cleaners on an inconspicuous piece of carpet, such as inside a closet.
- If a spill occurs, do something immediately. Don't wait.
- Using your white cloths, blot up as much of the stain as possible. Be very careful not to spread the stain. Work from the outside of the stain toward the middle to help prevent a ring. If you happen to have a wet/dry vacuum, you could use that.
- Treat the stain with the appropriate cleaner as mentioned above. Blot all excess moisture. Push the nap back to its original standing position. If the area is still very wet, stack some cloths on it and weigh it down.
- Be patient, the treatment may have to be repeated.

### Q. How can I remove existing pet urine odor from my carpet?

This is one of the most difficult problems to deal with. The thing is, it soaks right through the carpet into the pad and even under that to the flooring below. Unfortunately, most attempts to deal with this problem will only mask the odor temporarily. When we bought a house, it had this problem. We had the carpets professionally cleaned, but that wasn't good enough. We wanted to replace the carpets anyway, but wound up having to do it sooner than originally planned. Once the old carpet was ripped up, I thoroughly washed the plywood flooring with disinfectant cleaner in the offending area. After it had dried completely, we sealed the wood. Fresh new padding and carpet was installed. A lot of work, but we never had odor problems again. If you absolutely can't afford to have that room re-carpeted, do your best with a bacteria enzyme digester which you should find at your pet store. You may want to keep this on hand at all times for other emergencies. This also works on sour smells of an organic nature such as vomit and milk. You might also consider having the carpet in other rooms of the house professionally treated with soil retardant.

## General

*Q. I have sliding glass doors that lead to my patio. The glass is easy enough to clean, but how do I clean the tracks?*

I bet you thought it would be grand, having that big expanse of glass to gaze through. Probably nobody warned you of the aggravation inherent in this type of door. In fact, it's the same problem that shower door tracks and even multitrack windows pose. Because these doors lead to and from your patio, you probably get a fair amount of dirt, pebbles and twigs from the yard lodged in there. The thing is, you have to clean them frequently or the stuff builds up to a greasy goo and is very difficult to get out. To really get them clean you will have to get down on your hands and knees. Spray the track with an all-purpose cleaner, then use a thick white cloth, towel or diaper to clean. To get into corners, wrap the cloth around a screwdriver or other sturdy pointed object. Regular vacuuming or sweeping will help, but occasionally you will still have to get down on hands and knees to do a thorough job.

## COMPANY'S COMING

It's 4 P.M. and you're still in your housecoat. It's been a lazy day of sipping coffee, reading the newspaper, and yelling at the talk shows. When the phone rings, you assume it's your girlfriend. Wrong. It's Uncle Mel. He's passing through town and is only ten minutes away. He and his wife and seven kids would just love to stop by and catch up. Your choices are to:

a. Feign an accent. "Ia havea noa Uncle Mela. Youa gotta the wronga number." Then hang up and hide in the closet.
b. Pretend you have a bad connection. "Who is this? I can hardly hear you? Speak up. You're fading . . . fading . . ." Hang up and run for cover to your neighbor's house.
c. Pretend you lead an exciting life. "Uncle Mel — Fabulous to hear from you! Just on my way out the door. Dinner with Senator Snootbottom again! Ta, dear! Kissy kissy." Then go into your

prayer closet and ask for forgiveness or vow to get a life.
d. Put on some clothes and make the best of the situation.

If the thought of unexpected company strikes panic into your
soul, you need a plan for dealing with a messy house fast. Assuming
you are brave enough to face the music, here's some advice.

• Keep an emergency outfit handy. This would be one outfit that
is rarely worn, just saved for such emergencies. It could be a house
dress or nice jogging outfit.

• Consider which areas of the house company is most likely to
see. Probably the living room, possibly the kitchen, and almost certainly the bathroom. These are the areas to concentrate on. Forget
the unmade beds. There's no reason for them to enter the bedrooms
anyway.

• Get help. Gather all able family members and assign specific
jobs based on the suggestions below. Let's say you decided you would
like to entertain them in the living room. In that case, the living
room becomes top priority. After that is the bathroom and then the
kitchen. If possible, assign two people to the living room, one to the
kitchen, and one to the bath.

## The Living Room

• First, get rid of the clutter. (This could be an assigned job.)
• Grab a laundry basket and toss in the newspapers, magazines,
  toys, mail, dirty dishes, and any other odds and ends.
• Return the full basket to the laundry room and cover with a
  towel. Close the door.
• Return to the living room and remove all outerwear from the
  furniture. Quickly hang coats and shove shoes into closet or
  shoe basket. Bookbags and briefcases can be shoved into a
  nearby closet or quickly deposited in the owner's room.
• All of this should only take a few minutes if you put yourself
  into high gear.
• If you plan to dust, you'll have to gauge whether you have time
  to do a thorough job. A fully dusted room or a totally undusted
  room will be less noticeable than a half dusted room.
• If you are not sure you have time to dust, vacuum instead.

Unless you have the ideal carpet (one of those sculptured, multicolored sort of carpets that can go weeks without tattling) it is one of the most noticeable things in the room. Do a quick job; don't worry about every nook and cranny. Just get the main portion, the most visible part of the floor. If there's no time to vacuum, grab those dust bunnies and lint by hand instead.

- Spray lightly with room freshener and open a window if weather permits. Even if it is cold outside, crack a window for some fresh air.
- Open the curtains. Being able to look outside may take a bit of attention away from a less than perfect room.
- If it's nighttime, keep the lights low!

## The Bathroom
Again, deal first with the clutter.

- Grab towels and dirty clothes off the floor, shove tub toys into their basket or net.
- Clear the counters. If you have to, shove everything into drawers or under the sink—pray they won't peek.
- Grab a sponge and wipe the sink and counter area.
- Spray clean the mirror.
- Draw the shower curtain across the rod.
- You won't have time to scrub the toilet, so lift the lid and run some toilet paper around the rim of the bowl.
- If the shaggy commode covers or the throw rug look dirty and linty, remove them. Stuff them into the washing machine if you have to.
- Check that there is enough toilet tissue.
- Hang a clean towel on the rack.
- Spray lightly with air freshener.
- If there is a window in the bathroom, crack it.

## The Kitchen
If the kitchen is a really big mess, you won't have time to properly clean. You'll have to use the shove and hide method. Again, begin

with the clutter. Your main objective is to get the counters cleared and cleaned.

- Run a sink full of soapy water and place dishes, silverware and glasses inside. (A sink full of dishes isn't as bad as a counter covered with them. At least that way it looks like you are about to wash them and that things are under control.)
- Quickly return food to the refrigerator.
- Dirty pots and pans get shoved into the oven or dishwasher.
- Any odds and ends remaining on the counters get shoved somewhere: in the oven, in a cabinet, in the drawer under the oven, in the fridge or freezer, in the dishwasher, microwave, bread box, or whatever else you've got that will hide it.
- Wipe the counters with a sponge.
- Even if the floor is a mess, you won't have time to mop. You could run your vacuum over it or sweep if there's time.
- Simmer some cloves, cinnamon, or some other fragrant spice.

In all your hurrying, don't forget yourself. A little makeup and a comb through your hair will make you feel and look better. Even if the house isn't under perfect control, you can look as though you are.

If you are lucky, there will be family members there to help with this hurried housecleaning. If you are even luckier, or better yet, if you lay your four foundations, you'll never have to worry about unexpected company and a messy house.

## Emergency Cleaning Etiquette

- Don't overapologize. It just draws attention to the problem.
- Don't feel overly guilty. Everyone's house gets messy once in a while. It's not a crime.
- Don't make excuses. If you were simply feeling a bit lazier than usual, there's no need to fabricate some elaborate reason for the mess. You're entitled to goof off once in a while.

By the way, this hurried-up system also works when the house is a wreck and you just can't muster the strength to deal with it. *Pretend you've got company coming* (your mother-in-law?) and whiz around as fast as you can. You'll be amazed how much you can do in a short time. Give yourself twenty minutes to make a difference and you will.

*Chapter Twelve*

# BEFORE YOU BUY, BUILD OR REMODEL

I f you're like most people, you have a dream house. It may not exist in reality yet, but it does exist in your imagination. I've got a great one. Unfortunately, it's still in the fantasy stage.

If you are fortunate enough to be building your dream house, I'd like to point out a few small things that could keep your dream from becoming a nightmare.

Whether you choose to build a one-story ranch, a two-story traditional or a multilevel contemporary, a few key points can help. Here are my suggestions.

## Garages

• Garages should always lead into the kitchen, preferably through a mudroom. I feel the best situation is to have a mudroom for removing outerwear, a half bath and a pantry all arranged between garage and kitchen. Groceries can be carried directly to the pantry. Another nice touch is to have a pass-through window into the kitchen. In the kitchen, there is a counter directly below the window and the refrigerator is next to the counter. Perishables can be passed through and the fewest possible steps are taken.

• If financially feasible, you may want to have the length of the garage extended to accommodate a couple of storage rooms. One could be used for patio furniture, children's outdoor toys and so forth. Most people are hard put to find suitable storage for these items when winter comes. The storage room could be accessed from inside the garage, but should also have a back door leading to the yard for convenient unloading.

• In addition to that storage room, a second one could be set up as a box storage room. One of my first clients was in the process of building her dream house and she and her husband decided to do this. They have long since completed their home and are very happy with their box storage room.

• Since garage doors aren't usually noted for their beauty, you may want to see if it's possible to have yours facing to the side of the house rather than to the front.

## Kitchens

I have had every style imaginable and find the square or U-shaped the most convenient to use. Galley kitchens usually create too much traffic as they tend to lead from one place to another.

As for the arrangement, I like the sink and stove to be close to each other. If you locate them near the intersection of an L-shaped wall arrangement, they can be separated by a corner counter work-space. I find this works well. You will want to complete the work triangle with the refrigerator close by.

Islands are nice as long as they don't get in the way. However, don't locate your sink there or you'll constantly be dripping water as you reach toward the stove or refrigerator for something.

I also like a wide, deep counter for mixing ingredients and preparing foods for baking. If possible, locate deep bin-style drawers below this counter to store flour, sugar and other items.

If possible, before you begin building your dream kitchen, have an architect or design center lay it out for you on a computer that allows you to experience it through virtual reality. That way, you'll be sure to know if it's right for you.

## Laundry

What are you washing? For most of us, the vast majority of laundry items are articles of clothing. That being the case, it makes sense to locate the laundry room near the dirty clothes. Traditionally, laundry rooms have been located near the kitchen. This was fine in the days when women spent 80 percent of their days there. Now it just means doing a lot of unnecessary lugging around.

If you are planning a two-story house with bedrooms upstairs, have your laundry room built upstairs between the bedrooms. Since you are going to the trouble of building anyway, you may as well do it right and include a counter for folding, lots of wall cabinets for storage, and a clothes rod for hanging.

What about the possibility of two washers and dryers? Gets the job done in half the time. Or, one washer and two dryers. The dryers can be stacked for efficiency.

If possible, make the laundry room large enough to accommodate your sewing machine. You already have the counter which can be used for laying out and cutting fabric. You have a rod to hang works-in-progress and cabinets to store your supplies. While you do some mending, you can be washing fabric for shrinkage.

### Office

A small office located off the kitchen is a great treat. Meal planning, shopping lists and even bill paying can all be accomplished here instead of making a mess on the kitchen table. When coming home from shopping or work, receipts and paperwork can be dropped off quickly, before they get trailed throughout the house.

### BUYING NEW

In the past when you needed a new couch, refrigerator or kitchen sink, you probably made your decision based on what looked the prettiest or was on sale. Not bad reasons, surely. But now that you've learned to master housework, you know better than to fall for those gimmicks. *Anything* new can look pretty, but how long will it *stay* pretty and new-looking and how much work will it take? And what about bargains? Years of maintenance and upkeep will add much more to the original price.

Most rooms of the house are relatively low maintenance on their own. They are basic boxes with a couple of windows. All in all the most work will come from the items you choose to put in that room: the furniture, the carpets and the light fixtures. Fortunately there are many styles of furniture, appliances, fixtures and even carpeting available. Unfortunately many are manufactured more with aesthetics in mind than maintenance. Anything that is aesthetically pleasing will not last without the proper maintenance. Luckily, some designers do consider the beleaguered homeowners and give us credit for being a bit more than cleaning machines.

There are however, two rooms of the house that are far more

demanding. The kitchen and the bathroom are often the busiest rooms. In near continuous use, they especially need to be low maintenance for the sake of our sanity.

So, before you bring one more item into your newly hallowed halls, consider the real cost: the cost of maintenance, your time and energy. So, whether you are building, remodeling or just replacing something, here's what to look for.

## KITCHENS

This is arguably the busiest and most important room in the house. There is something about a kitchen that draws us. Even when it is not necessary to be there, we often are. Children do homework there, we often socialize there, we make plans, share meals, daydream all within these walls. The kitchen is truly the heart of the home and the hub of activity. It also unfortunately represents enormous amounts of work. In order to spend more time sipping coffee with friends and less time scrubbing, you can choose appliances, floor coverings and even cabinets that require the minimum amount of maintenance.

### Cabinets.

Cabinets and floors are probably the most noticeable things in your kitchen. Everyone wants pretty cabinets, but some are much harder to care for than others. Basically you want a smooth face. A flat vertical surface will not allow dust to settle in corners and protrusions. It will be easier to wipe clean and will look better longer. Of course, so much of this has to do with personal tastes. If you like the European-style cabinets which are very popular now, that would be a good choice. They are available with a vinyl coating or laminate, have a flat surface, and don't require hardware to open and close. If you must have a wood cabinet, look for a sleek design. Don't choose one in a darkly stained finish as this will show too many specks. If possible, eliminate the need for hardware by choosing drawers with slanted or beveled edges. If you prefer to have drawer and cabinet pulls, choose simple round knobs. Anything too ornate will be a pain to clean.

### Soffits.

If you are building a new home, be sure your builder does not leave an open space between the top of the cabinets and the ceiling.

Having this space only causes extra work because the cabinet tops collect greasy kitchen dust. To eliminate this work, you have two choices. You could have soffits built above the cabinet, or you could have extra long cabinets installed. Soffits are simply drywall built so that it is flush with the face of the cabinet. The other choice is the taller cabinets. This is a good choice for many, especially those with limited storage space. The highest shelf can be used for seldom-used items.

### Counters.

It seems to me that the two most popular choices for kitchen counter tops are the laminated (Formica) surfaces and solid core (corian). Of the two, I see the formica used more often. It comes in a wide variety of colors and patterns, is very resilient (though not indestructible), and is much cheaper than the solid core alternative. Either works well, is easy to care for, and will take a lot of punishment. Other possibilities include tile (seen in upscale houses and some older homes) and stainless steel, which is a companion to the restaurant-style stoves, ovens and refrigerators now making their way into homes. Tile is pretty to look at, but is too much bother. Both the tiles and the grout can chip and the grout can stain. Stainless steel is very strong and the brushed style is relatively easy to maintain. If you don't mind the institutional look, you may like it very much. For most people and purposes the formica counters will be the wisest choice. Be sure to choose a style with a pattern and avoid dark solid colors. These will prove too difficult to keep looking clean. A pattern in neutral colors will hide spots and streaks and may do a better job disguising nicks and scratches.

### Sinks.

I have had both stainless steel and porcelain sinks. I love the stainless steel, hate the porcelain. Stainless steel (which by the way *can* stain) is inexpensive, easy to care for and very durable. If you make this choice, buy one close to the top of the line in quality. Also, be sure you have one that is deep enough to keep water in. I like the double-sided style myself. Porcelain looks beautiful in the showroom but is an incredible pain in the kitchen. Gently rest a pot in the sink and you've got seventeen ugly gray streaks. If you ever chip the thing you have to either replace it (*very* costly) or patch it. Patching will look tacky if you do it and will be costly if you have a professional do it.

### Flooring.

Aside from cabinets, the floor is the most noticeable thing in the kitchen. It takes a lot of abuse and needs to be easy to care for. Since this is a room where practicality counts, avoid the trendy styles you may see in home decor magazines. I've seen everything from brick, tile and carpet to a gray vinyl resembling Leggo building blocks. I've had just about everything and the hands-down winner is sheet vinyl. It's easy to care for, looks good for years, and won't cost a fortune. Because you won't have the seams that you would with tile or vinyl blocks, it will be easier to clean and keep looking clean. When you choose the style, try a pattern in a medium color or colors and smooth finish. Avoid the foam-backed version which will puncture easily.

### Appliances.

Since these are an important investment that you will live with for years, you have to choose carefully to get what you want.

If you are building, or doing extensive remodeling, you may want to consider having your appliances built in. This means only the face of the appliance shows, drastically reducing upkeep. Also, dishwashers, trash compactors and refrigerators can be disguised by having front panels that match your cabinets. If you don't choose built-ins, be careful about the color choice you do make. I like almond the best. It gives a clean, warm appearance and isn't as difficult to keep clean as stark white or dark-colored appliances.

### The stove.

Since your stove is the messiest appliance, you will want to stick with one that is easy to clean. That means flat surfaces, no knobs and no black. If you are buying a new stove, you may be interested in the drop-in (cooktop) style which is separate from the oven. These provide for a cabinet below, keeping pots and pans close at hand. Since coils and the burner pans below are such a problem to keep clean, you may want to choose a flat surface style with enclosed coils. They are very easy to wipe clean when cool. Another thing to avoid when possible is the knob. There are now styles available with touch pad controls (similar to microwave ovens) that eliminate knobs, which are extremely difficult to clean around.

### The oven.

Choose a self-cleaning oven. If you have never used one, you are really missing out. They are great, *well* worth the extra cost.

### The refrigerator.

Get a frost-free freezer with your refrigerator. Aside from that, you will want an orange peel finish which eliminates the fingerprint problem. I like the way the side-by-side style looks, but I'm not crazy about the way many of them function. Large items such as holiday turkeys are hard to fit in the narrower compartments. Some manufacturers are providing more space. Either the side-by-side or freezer on top version offers dispensers for water and ice. Aside from the outer appearance, you will want to consider how the inside functions. Newer styles usually have lots of compartments and drawers. Test them out to see how easy they are to remove. Consider how wide the door will open. Will it be next to a wall, limiting its ability to open when removing shelves and drawers for cleaning? Do you have a preference in shelf style? Wire rack styles allow spills to drip all the way to the bottom, while clear plastic shelves will catch the spills, but will look messier and need more upkeep.

### Small appliances.

This is where people often get carried away, buying every new gadget that comes on the market. I suggest you severely limit small appliances, as relatively few are actually used. If you are among those who do put all your little gadgets to good use, I suggest you keep your counters as clear as possible by using the suspended versions that mount under cabinets. Of course, not everything is available in this style, but do what you can to help yourself. I have seen coffee makers, can openers, radios, knife racks and cookbook holders all available in this mounted style.

## BATHROOMS

The items you clean the most are the sink and faucet, toilet and tub. For the sake of your sanity, they should be easy to clean, without requiring undue amounts of special pampering.

### The sink.

You may be surprised at the variety of choices there are for just this one item. What you want is a sink deep enough that water stays in rather than sloshes out, one devoid of molded soap bar holders, and one in a neutral color, or better yet, neutral colors in a marbled swirl. I like the sinks that are molded sink/counter/backsplash combinations. These seem easier to clean because everything is in one piece. The marbled effect helps hide spots between cleanings. Another advantage of molded sinks is that they usually have a slight slope so that water runs back to the sink, rather than off the counter onto the floor. There is no metal ring to clean or to scrape gunk out from under. A different choice is pedestal sinks, which have made a resurgence in popularity. These work well when coupled with wall cabinets and can really help eliminate the counter clutter problem.

### The faucet.

You want something that is easy to clean as well as easy to operate with wet hands. A brushed finish is the easiest maintenance. Who has time to polish chrome? Also, consider the style, commonly used in kitchens, that has just one lever to adjust water flow and temperature. You may even like one that swings out of the way. The one lever style is easier to operate and certainly easier to clean than the separate knobs. Always look for the sleekest designs, avoiding extra frills such as carvings, indentations or wood. If you decide to go with knobs, test them out and imagine what they will be like with wet hands. Too round and smooth will mean too slick and hard to operate when hands are wet. I also suggest you avoid knobs or handles with wood which may take a beating from water and will only compound the cleaning problem by combining surfaces to clean.

### The vanity.

If you forego a pedestal sink and decide on a vanity, be sure to get one with drawers. The extra expense is worth it because a vanity that consists of just one large cupboard is nearly useless. It's difficult to keep organized and has lots of wasted space. As always, keep in mind the cost of upkeep. Some of the fancy wood vanities are beautiful to look at, but will have to be cared for almost like a piece of furniture with dusting and polishing. You may prefer to choose an easy care laminate that only needs occasional wiping down with a damp cloth. If possible, have a piece of laminate installed on the bottom of the cabinet. This will help prevent water damage in the event of a leak and will prove easy to wipe clean. Also, have a shelf installed so that the upper space can be put to good use.

### The tub/shower.

From a cleaning point of view, I'm all for the newer molded tub/ shower units. With no grout to scrub and tiles to crack, chip and replace, they really cut down on maintenance worries. They aren't as tough as the old cast iron-style tubs that I grew up with, so you will have to use care and a nonabrasive cleaner.

If however, you are a diehard who loves the look of tile, consider using tiles sized larger than 4¼". This will mean less grout surface and fewer possibilities for mildew and chipping. If you tile, use neutrals whenever possible. Find a tub in the same color (cast iron porcelain tubs are still the best). I love the look of emerald green or midnight blue tubs, but I know lime buildup and water spots would be a nightmare.

If you go for the molded unit, look for one with smooth lines, a center bar for balancing, and a minimum number of indented shelves (meant to stow shampoo). More than is necessary will mean more work.

### Shower doors/curtains.

As for shower doors on tubs, I personally hate them. They are such a bother to clean, get lime buildups, and the runners are a pain. If the doors are mirrored, that's another category of aggravation. The only other choice is a shower curtain, which has a few moldy drawbacks. Between these choices, you have to choose what you consider to be the lesser of two evils. I would suggest a good quality curtain that is hung on the rod with a cheap liner. The inexpensive liner can be replaced periodically rather than be cleaned, and will allow the prettier, better-quality curtain to stay clean. Hang them high enough that the bottoms don't stand in soapy water from a slow drain.

### The toilet.

The concern for water conservation has caused manufacturers to reevaluate toilet design. I have yet to see the self-cleaning model (which I hope is just around the corner), but at least some small improvements have been made. I think the hardest part of cleaning a toilet is the base. They have deep grooves and those obnoxious little caps that seem to spend more time floating around the bathroom floor than covering the fastening bolts. Look for a toilet with the sleekest base possible. In fact, there are even suspended toilets that eliminate the base entirely, but these are better installed in new construction. Your choice should be one with a sleek design (some are now made with small tank, bowl and base all in one unit, reducing some of the work), and one in a neutral color.

### The floor covering.

I've had both ceramic tile and vinyl flooring and I think vinyl is easier to maintain. I recommend sheet vinyl. With fewer seams to deal with, the sheet style will be easier to clean and maintain. A neutral color scheme with a random pattern will help hide spots. You may also want to consider running the floor cover up a little on the wall, called coving. This will eliminate the need for a baseboard and will make mopping a cinch. The corners will be tricky, so let a professional do it. It will look different than what you're used to, but you will love it for its easy maintenance. I don't recommend wall-to-wall carpet. It may be cozy on cold winter mornings, but will prove to be a nightmare if there is any problem with an overflowing toilet.

### The mirror.

When we were younger and less experienced, we had a big mirror cut to fit over the sink in one of our homes. It was great for grooming, but a nightmare for toothpaste specks and water spots. If you install a mirror, make sure you place it high enough over the sink to miss all that flying toothpaste. If you need a big mirror for grooming, get a long one to install on the back of the door or some other place away from the line of fire. A cleaning cloth can be stowed under the vanity and the mirror can easily be cleaned with a few swipes. You don't even need to use glass cleaner if the bathroom is still a little moist from shower use. It only takes a few seconds but makes a big difference. If you want a mirror/cabinet combination, avoid chrome cabinets. They are a pain to keep clean. They even get rusty on the inside. It's better to spend a little more up front then be paying for frugality for the next twenty years.

## AROUND THE HOUSE

### Light Fixtures

Talk about choices. Choosing kitchen and bath appliances will be a snap compared to choosing lighting. You can save your sanity if you follow some basic principles.

• First of all, what do you want to accomplish with your light fixtures? You want to bring light to an area or a room. Therefore, the purpose is to light the area, not decorate it with high mainte-nance lamps, chandeliers and fixtures. Go for the sleek designs.

• Whenever possible, make use of natural light. Natural light is the most pleasant, cheapest, and seems to have a better effect on people than artificial lighting. One of the houses we lived in had skylights on every level. They were wonderful, extremely low mainte-nance, and the natural daylight they provided kept me in a better mood. If you're building or doing extensive remodeling, I strongly suggest you consider skylights.

• Atmosphere is important, and some people simply prefer the warmer glow of lamps and wall-mounted lights to that of the over-head fixtures. Even if you do want lamps, it's a good idea to have overhead lighting installed because there are times when lamps sim-ply do not provide enough light.

Your basic lighting options are floor and table lamps, wall-mounted fixtures, ceiling lights, overhead track and recessed lights, and hanging lights.

## Floor and table lamps.

This sort of lighting allows you to create warm, cozy spots of light. Of the two, I suggest floor lamps when possible. This may eliminate the need for end tables and that alone should reduce some of your work. A big drawback to both floor and table lamps are, of course, the cords. You can purchase devices that will hold the excess cord inside, perhaps slightly reducing the chance of tripping over a loose cord. If you do decide to use these sorts of lamps, look for styles that have very sleek features. Nooks and crannies capture dust. Also, be choosy about the shade. Anything heavily pleated or with fabric folds will be unnecessarily difficult to keep clean. Smooth clean lines are always easiest. Be sure to select a lamp with balanced weight. A top-heavy lamp will topple easily. Better to have it a bit bottom heavy.

## Wall-mounted lights.

These are similar to lamps in that they allow for a cozy spot of light, but aren't well-suited for general-purpose lighting. Don't use these thinking you can forego overhead lights. As for choosing fixtures, use the same principles for easy maintenance: sleek design, nothing overly ornate. Also, avoid styles with etching or that combine materials such as wood and glass. All of these make for more difficult cleaning.

## Track and recessed lighting.

Both of these are ceiling lights that allow light to be focused on particular areas in the room. I've had both and liked both very much. However, the track lighting does require more maintenance than the recessed style because the track itself and the mounted units get dusty. Recessed lights come in a variety of styles, including cylindrical and round.

## Ceiling lights.

I grew up in an older home and every room had ceiling lights. Each one was covered with those curved glass covers known as bowl lights. I hate bowl lights. Even in our modern world you still see them and every piece of dust and flying bug from the neighborhood in them. If you have this type of overhead lighting, it's better to use a light cover that will enclose the bulb. If it must be open, have one that is open at the bottom so bug corpses will slide their way out and down to cleaning level.

### Hanging lights.

Commonly used in dining rooms and eat-in kitchens, these are good candidates for other areas of the home as well. If you are fortunate enough to be building a home, you could build in hanging lights. They are low maintenance because they don't require a table to sit on, you don't have to move them around to clean under them, and they have no cords to trip over. If you choose this style, choose the sleekest style with the smoothest bulb cover or shade available. An alternative for an existing home is the swag lamp. Some of these, however, are very ornate, so you may have to shop around a bit to find one with low-maintenance features.

### Area lights.

If you are building a new home, you may want your architect or builder to include area lights in some specific locations. For instance, do you like to read in bed? Where in the bedroom will your bed sit? Have a wall-mounted area light set in place above your bed. Another popular type of area light (also called task lighting) is the under cabinet light used in kitchens. Not only does it provide a cozy glow, it gives you light exactly where you need it.

### Chandeliers.

Unless you have a maid (and don't like her very much), avoid the chandelier. They are simply too much trouble.

## Floors

There are some beautiful floors that anyone could fall for, if they didn't take ease of maintenance into consideration. Floors are a huge chunk of your housekeeping labor. Knowing which sorts of floors to have and *where* can greatly reduce your effort.

Basically there are two categories of floor: hard floors such as brick, tile, wood and vinyl, and soft floors such as area rugs and wall-to-wall carpeting.

Common sense tells us that there are certain places in a home that require hard flooring, while others are better suited to soft flooring. There are a few places that could go either way. Here's how to decide:

### Consider the source — the water source.

If you are unsure whether a room should have hard or soft flooring, think of it this way. Is there a water source in this room? Is there any possibility of a leak? If you answered yes, then you need a water-proof, hard floor surface there. For rooms like kitchens, bathrooms, laundry rooms and utility rooms, I suggest sheet vinyl. It's better than vinyl tile, easy to care for and not too expensive. One word of warning though: avoid the foam-backed style. High heels and other sharp objects will poke holes in it.

### Where's the wood?

I grew up in a home with hardwood maple floors. They were beautiful. I still love wood floors, but don't find them practical for every room. Wood is ideal for foyers, reception halls and formal dining rooms. You *don't* want wood where you want a warmer, cozier feel. If you put wood floors in your living room, then use an area rug to cozy up the place, you have defeated your low maintenance goals. You will have two different floors to care for and besides that, area rugs are bothersome. They are difficult to vacuum because they get caught in the vacuum. Use wood flooring where it will be used alone.

The proper type of hardwood floor, maple or oak, will hold up for many years and be a beautiful addition to your home. Avoid any sort of soft wood (pine or fir) which will not hold up as well. For proper maintenance, it's essential that wood be sealed with urethane. This will protect the wood and allow you to do damp mopping. You have to be careful not to use too much water with wood. It can get between cracks and cause buckling.

### Wall-to-wall comfort.

Carpet is the floor of choice when you want a warm atmosphere. Living and family rooms, bedrooms, studies, all are suited to wall-to-wall carpet. I always recommend this type of carpet over area rugs because, as I said, area rugs are just too difficult to vacuum.

For the past twenty years wall-to-wall carpeting has been a standard feature in new home construction. However, not all carpets are created equal. The best carpet for homes with families (or people looking for low maintenance) is the multilevel, sculptured carpet. It hides foot marks, dirt, lint, spots, stains, and probably even some things you don't want to know about. It is available in different multicolored schemes.

Beautiful plush (uniform length pile) carpets look elegant and sophisticated in magazines or model homes. The problem is that they won't remain that way for long, especially in the high-traffic zones. If you insist on plush in low traffic zones, such as the master bedroom, at least choose a medium color. I can say from personal experience that light and dark colors will be slave drivers. And, consider the fact that although the bedroom is low traffic compared to other areas in the house, you will still have zones (from the bed to the bathroom — from the bathroom to the closet) that will show wear much faster than others.

Alternative flooring such as ceramic tile, brick and cork are too much bother to consider. I've had ceramic tile, and it's just too much trouble. Brick and cork have their place, but not on the floors inside a family home. Stick to the three basics, wood, wall-to-wall carpet and sheet vinyl. Use them in the places as suggested and I think you'll be as satisfied as possible.

## Furniture

As with everything else in our homes, furniture is supposed to be there for our convenience. Quite often, we make the mistake of putting appearance before function. I will concede that it is not always easy to find both function and beauty but you should exercise all options to do so. If you don't you will pay for it later. Let's look at some basic principles:

• Before buying, consider exactly how this piece of furniture will be used, where exactly you will put it in your home, and how often you will have to clean, plump, wash, polish, dust or wax it.

• When buying fabric furniture, such as couches and chairs, always go for a medium-colored fabric, preferably in a print. Dark and light solids will show every thread, fuzzball and animal hair.

• Give thought to the stamina of the fabric. I loved my southwestern cotton sofa, but it did require more maintenance than its predecessor, a synthetic weave. Generally, synthetics such as nylon, Dacron and rayon will hold up better than natural fabrics.

• When possible, buy couches and chairs that sit right on the floor. This eliminates the need to vacuum underneath.

• You may want to purchase the style of sofa and chair that has pillows attached. Lots of furniture now comes in the loose pillow style, which may prove bothersome to others.

• Try not to mix materials. Avoid fabric sofas with wood trim. The wood will have to be polished or oiled—a hazard, with fabric so close.

• Resist anything with tufts. It may look cute in the store, but the buttons will pop and dust will collect in all those little valleys. Always look for sleek, smooth lines. If necessary, imagine yourself at home, cleaning the piece. That should help you resist troublesome pieces.

### Wood furniture.

Much of the furniture in your home will be wood. Dining tables and chairs, end and coffee tables, and bedroom sets are all usually wood. Finished hardwoods are fine for these things. I don't recommend soft wood such as pine. I had a pine bed once. It was beautiful, but every swipe of the vacuum dented it. I also don't recommend unfinished wood. It will absorb stains readily. Make sure any wood furniture you purchase has been sealed.

### Alternative furniture.

Someone finally figured out that children need lower maintenance furniture than adults. I've seen some wonderful bedroom sets for children that have a laminate finish. It's durable, easy to clean, won't require painting or polishing, and won't dent like wood.

### Built-in furniture.

If you are building a home, you may as well build in a little furniture as well. Actually, I think some built-in furniture is fine, while other things just aren't worthwhile. In bedrooms plan an extra-large closet and have drawers built in. Why bother polishing dressers and chests?

A fairly typical built-in is the breakfast nook. I have mixed feelings about these. When I was growing up, a friend had a painted wood one in her kitchen. It was easy enough to clean; however, if you build one with vinyl seats, crumbs will make their way between cushions or between the wall and cushions and will be difficult to remove.

In a TV room or family room, I suggest built-in cabinets for storing videocassette tapes. The shelves don't have to be very deep, but you should definitely have doors to reduce dusting.

In a playroom, built-in cabinets and drawers are great for toy and game storage.

## ARMED AND DANGEROUS

These suggestions should help next time you go shopping. Armed with this knowledge, I'm sure you'll make the proper decisions.

*Chapter Thirteen*

# TOO POOPED? PAY!

I f you have ever dreamed of having a maid, it may be time to get one. There's a lot to be said for this ultimate homemaker's fantasy.

If you do take the plunge and hire a maid, you should still continue working on organizing your home. It will make things easier for you between maid visits, and it will certainly make things easier for the maid. It may even save you money because the less clutter she has to deal with, the less time she'll have to spend cleaning.

However, if you do decide to take this stroll down life's path to carefree housecleaning, you may wind up tripping over a few stumbling blocks. Let me offer some guidance.

## WHY YOU SHOULD HIRE A HOUSECLEANER

You can probably think of a dozen reasons why you would like to have a housecleaner, but I bet you also have a haunting reason why you wouldn't.

### I Can't Afford It

Only you know if you can afford to hire help. However, consider the other conveniences on which you spend your money. According to the National Restaurant Association, in 1990 the average American spent 42.5 percent of their food dollars *away* from home. That's a lot of eating out. That compares to 25 percent in 1955. Many consider this more than merely convenient; it's essential. Busy schedules demand a compromise between convenience and expense. Likewise, housecleaning services come down to a matter of priority. If it's important enough, you'll budget for it. You have to decide if the convenience outweighs the cash outlay.

Considering that your housecleaner may charge by the hour, you may be able to modify your actual expenditure by assigning only the most difficult jobs to the housecleaner and doing the others yourself. Another money-saving possibility is to have the housecleaner come every other week. Even if you do the work on alternate weeks, this system still cuts your work in half.

Regardless of how often you want the work done, you should have the prospective housecleaner give you a bid on the job. They could come to your house and give you an estimate based on your list of requirements.

### If I Get a Cleaning Person, They'll Know What a Messy Person I Really Am

If you are worried about that, forget it. That's what keeps them in business and for them to find fault with a messy client is biting the hand that feeds them.

### If I Get a Housecleaner, It'll Just Be Out of laziness. I Do Have Time to Clean, I Just Hate to

If you think you'll be racked with guilty feelings for employing a cleaning person, let me reassure you: The feelings will probably go away after about five minutes. Everyone can use a little help now and then. If your life is demanding enough, give yourself a break. In just a few hours a week, a professional can make your home and your family's life more comfortable. You can use that time to catch up on other things, goof off or shop. Your disposition may even change for the better and your family will surely like that.

## HOW TO CHOOSE A HOUSECLEANER

If you have never used a housecleaner before, you may have no clue about how to choose one. It's not simple. There are many things to consider. First, how do you find prospective candidates? Exercise all your options. Scan the yellow pages (under janitorial services as well as housecleaning services) and bulletin boards at local stores, query friends and neighbors, and even call churches and other buildings that would employ such cleaners.

You may encounter such candidates as the typical freelance cleaning lady (or man) who works alone, husband and wife teams, college students, or you deal with a business that specifically employs cleaning personnel.

In any event, you should be aware of the differences between hiring that nice college student who wants to make a little pocket money and using an established maid service that trains and pays the cleaners themselves.

Remember Zoe Baird? (President Clinton's first nominee for attorney general.) She and her husband had hired a couple as nanny/chauffeur/housekeepers. As employers they did not pay social security for these people and she was forced to resign the nomination. Even if you don't think you'll be nominated to the Cabinet any time soon, you need to be aware of your obligations concerning the hiring of people who will work around your home.

Basically, you are required to pay social security taxes for anyone working in and around your home, if the pay is $50 or more per quarter (every three months). That means the maid who comes once a week, the babysitter who comes every Tuesday and Thursday and so forth. You may find that some freelance housecleaners do *not* want you to pay their social security taxes. This is because they do not want their income reported. You are required by law, however, so be sure to hire someone who will cooperate with you on this matter.

I have been told that at this writing there is a change in process regarding the way you file. However, I can tell you this: If you call the Internal Revenue Service at (800) 829-3676, and ask for publication #926 "Employer taxes for household employees," it will tell you what you need to know. You may decide to withhold taxes from their checks (current rate 7.65 percent) or, you may decide to pay both your share and the employee's (15.3 percent). These taxes are to be paid quarterly, so don't confuse them with filing your own income taxes once a year.

Of course, your accountant should also be able to give you the latest information regarding the requirements.

At any rate, the choice of who to hire is entirely yours and may come down to personality. You may make your choice based solely on who you trust the most and with whom you feel most comfortable. I wouldn't discourage you from dealing one-on-one with someone who has been recommended or someone you trust. However, some people will undoubtedly find it easier to deal with the businesses that employ, train, and pay social security taxes for their employees (the housecleaners) just as any other business does. If you decide to forego these businesses and find someone who freelances, be certain to speak with your accountant and the IRS about filing the proper forms.

It may seem ridiculous to you to have to pay social security for someone who only spends a few hours a week in your home. However, it is the law and ignoring it means breaking it. For purely selfish reasons you need to uphold the law because there are consequences. (Just ask Baird.) In addition, there is the matter of workman's comp in the event of an injury sustained by the housecleaner, though the rules on this vary from state to state. Do it by the book. Check with your accountant and get the publication I suggested from the IRS. If all of this seems like too much of a hassle, work with one of those businesses that employ housecleaners. Be certain that they actually do pay for those things and do not act solely as a referral service.

Once you have a list of potential candidates, interview them. You could do this over the phone if you'd rather not have someone in your home until you have checked them out. If working through a cleaning business, ask if their employees are bonded. Don't assume they are. Also, ask how long they have been in business and what training they have. A homemaker with fifteen years experience cleaning her own home may be just as good as someone working for a specialty business.

Always get references. Any reputable freelancer would be happy to supply references. Even someone new to housecleaning could supply letters from people familiar with their character and dependability. Get at least two or three.

Next, follow up on the references. Many people mistakenly think the letter of reference is, in itself, assurance. Believing this, some wind up telling horror stories of disastrous consequences. These things are easy enough for the unscrupulous person to dummy up. Creating a fictional name and background is very easy to do, so follow up on all references. Make sure the person offering the reference is a real person and that they themselves are reputable. It's easy for one crook to get another to give a glowing reference.

If you have any qualms about the ability of the person you choose, tell them you would like to begin this on a trial basis. They should agree to come and clean for one or two weeks and then let you make up your mind if this really is something you want to do. This will make it easier for you to stop the service if you decide they aren't satisfactory.

## WHAT TO EXPECT FROM YOUR HOUSECLEANER

I have noticed that many problems occur in life due to misunderstandings between parties. Usually this happens when results differ because one or both parties failed to communicate their expectations.

A case in point is that of the disgruntled homemaker who hired a maid and then did not call her back because she felt she hadn't done a good job. "She left so many things undone. She didn't wash any clothes, she left my husband's pile of change, papers and other junk on his dresser and she didn't even put my kid's toys away. Why should I pay for that?"

Before entering into any agreement with a housecleaner, be sure they understand exactly what you want and are *willing* to comply. In fact, a contract wouldn't hurt. Some will be willing to do basic cleaning like dusting, polishing and mopping floors. You may also want them to wash windows, clean out the fireplace, do dishes and clean the oven. Don't assume that they will do *anything*. Always ask up front if there are any particular things that they are unwilling to do, even occasionally.

I think it was unfair of the homemaker above to expect her cleaning person to do organizing and general pickup. They are there to *clean*. Unless they have specifically agreed to straighten as well, do not expect it. You should get the clutter out of their way and let them clean. This means picking up odds and ends from the carpets you expect them to vacuum. It means clearing off the dressers you want them to polish and clearing towels off the bathroom floor you want them to scrub.

The homemaker above was unhappy because expectations were not clearly defined. Most housecleaners do not expect to do laundry. They would think it presumptuous on their parts to go rummaging through closets, under beds and in hampers to collect dirty clothes. If you want this done, ask your cleaner if he would be willing. If he says no, then send the laundry out. Most attendant-supervised

Laundromats will wash and fold laundry and charge either a flat fee or by the pound. They will even do ironing for a fee.

And what about the problem of pocket items left out on the dresser? A cleaning person would have to know a family inside and out to know where to put the change and what to do with the papers and gum. They should have permission to open drawers to put things away. As for the toys, it's the same situation. Do you have a clearly defined and recognizable system for toy storage? If not, how can the cleaner be expected to put things in their proper place when they don't really have a proper place?

There is a difference between straightening and cleaning, so make sure you are both clear on expectations. You do the pickup, let them do the actual cleaning.

## ESTABLISHING THE ROUTINE

Once you have chosen a cleaning person and are clear on what they will or will not do, it would be wise to establish a regular routine of tasks. For instance, on each visit you may want them to dust in every room, polish the wood furniture, scrub the bathrooms, mop the kitchen floor, and vacuum all the carpets. If you keep this as the standard, they will probably only improve and get faster over time as they develop a rhythm to their routine.

Occasionally you will have seasonal work that you will want done. That is, assuming you have already discussed this and they are willing. This work could be done in addition to their regular routine, or in lieu of it if they do not have the time. At any rate, specify exactly what it is you would like done. Your cleaning person is not a mind reader, so don't expect them to just see what needs to be done. Make a list, even if you are usually present.

Most cleaning people prefer to have a regular time slot for doing your house. This allows them to make plans and schedule other jobs as well. It's also preferable for you since you will be able to relax, knowing when things will get done.

Also, even if you have a particular way of cleaning things, your housecleaner will no doubt have one as well. As long as the results are essentially the same, don't quibble over methods.

## Odds and Ends

• Be sure it is clearly understood whose cleaning products and equipment will be used. Some cleaners may have certain preferred brands and may even want to bring their own vacuum, mop and cleaning rags. This should all be included in the price. If you would prefer your own particular brands be used, be sure to specify this and make sure to always have them in stock.

• If they use your vacuum, be sure it is in good repair at all times. It will just be a waste of your money and their time if they have to fight with a temperamental vacuum. Of course, always have a few spare bags in the same location and since I seem to go through belts about as quickly as bags, I always have at least two or three in stock as well.

• Always be considerate about informing your housecleaner about any vacations or other periods of time when their service will not be necessary. This is how they make their living and even an occasional cancellation may hurt them financially. Consider having them do other types of cleaning while you are on vacation — wash walls or windows. They will appreciate your concern for their income.

Also, give them plenty of notice if you will be needing them more often then usual.

• Pets — if you have one or more pets, be sure the housecleaner knows what is expected while they are in the house. Is it OK to let the cat out? Can the dog go in the garage? Leave reminder notes since yours is probably not the only house being cleaned and everyone has memory lapses.

• Extra-delicate items — if you have some delicate items that are particularly precious to you, you may want to excuse the housecleaner from responsibility for those items. Let them know that they don't have to clean those, or better yet, put them in a safe place before the person arrives.

• Don't get underfoot — if you will be home during the hours your cleaning person will be working, don't get underfoot! Professionals don't need someone looking over their shoulder every minute and they don't need the distraction.

• It's good to have an understanding about what is permissible for them to do when you are not there to supervise. Is it alright if they eat your food, drink your coffee, use your phone, play your stereo, take a lunch break?

• Be aware of time spent — if you will be present during the cleaning sessions and until you grow to trust your housecleaner, try to be aware of how much time they are spending on individual tasks. For instance, if it takes you less than ten minutes to scrub your bathroom (excluding mopping) your housecleaner shouldn't be spending forty minutes on the job.

## Things to Get Clear Before They Start Working for You

In the interest of peace, it would behoove you to have a written agreement about certain things before you actually hire someone. Things to cover include:

### Broken items.

You should have a written agreement regarding what happens in the event of breakage. Does the cleaning company pay for it? What if it's an individual? Do they pay? Always check with your insurance agent to see if your homeowner's policy will cover the cost. Even if they do cover breakage by cleaning persons, you will likely have to cover the deductible. Who pays that?

### Cancellations and no-shows.

From the outset you should have an agreement on what action to take if this happens. Naturally, everyone gets sick, so be fair and understanding. However, if your cleaning person is sick every other week, a change should be made. Let them know you depend on them and if they can't be there most of the time, you will make other arrangements. If they simply don't show up without calling, ask if they will do their next scheduled appointment at half price. Likewise, if you forget to cancel and they show up with supplies in hand, consider offering to pay at least half for their trouble. If you are satisfied with your cleaning person, it is worthwhile to keep a harmonious relationship.

### Giving them a key.

This can be a very tough situation. If you will not be present during cleanings, you will have to make some sort of arrangement for letting them in. It's usually risky to hide a key. If you have a trusted neighbor who is *always* home at the time of the appointment, that's a good choice. However, those sorts of homebodies are hard to find these days. Of course, you could give your cleaning person a key if you feel comfortable doing so. If you do, ask them not to mark it in any way. If they have several customers and a house key for each on a big ring, and each key tagged with the client's address, it could be a disaster if lost. They could use an alternate way of coding the keys by using the colored covers that fit on the key. Of course, they still have to remember which color belongs to whom. If you give your key to a cleaning company, ask how keys are identified. Keys should not be tagged because they too are vulnerable to loss or theft.

### Substitutions.

If you are working through a cleaning company and you have a regular cleaner assigned to your house, ask what they do in the event that person is sick. They may be able to offer a substitute if that is suitable to you. If not, let them know that you would prefer to skip the cleaning when your regular is unavailable. Occasionally a free-lancer may be sick and want to send a friend or family member. Again, be clear on this up front. If you are uncomfortable letting an unfamiliar person into your house, it's certainly your right to refuse.

### Occasional cleaning.

Even if you decide not to have housecleaning done on a regular basis, you may still want help occasionally. A thorough spring or fall cleaning, holiday cleaning or other occasional cleaning may be in order. Most of the janitorial and housecleaning services I spoke to did indeed offer such occasional help. I suggest you still sign a contract. Just in case they accidentally break something, you'll be covered.

I know I have given you a lot of things to consider. Don't let that dissuade you from pursuing this luxury. Just think how wonderful it will be once the details are ironed out!

Here's a sample housecleaning contract. If you want to use something like this, check with your lawyer to be sure all details are covered.

## HOUSECLEANING AGREEMENT

| Client | Housecleaner |
|---|---|
| Name _____ | Name _____ |
| Address _____ | Address _____ |
| Phone # _____ | Phone # _____ |
| | SS # _____ - _____ - _____ |

The following is an agreement between _____ (client) of _____(address) and _____ (housecleaner) of _____ (address) hereinafter known as the Client and the Housecleaner. It is agreed that beginning on _____ (date) the Housecleaner will perform the services stated below on _____ (for instance, Mondays from 9:00 A.M. until no later than 12:00 noon). These services include _____ (dusting all rooms, vacuuming the carpets and scrubbing both bathrooms). Said Housecleaner has agreed to occasionally perform other services when requested. These additional but occasional services include _____ (washing windows, polishing wood tables and doing laundry). Client agrees to pay Housecleaner _____ per hour for services rendered or _____ for the entire job, regardless of the amount of time it takes. In the event the Housecleaner does not arrive for the regular appointment, and has offered no warning of such cancellation, the Housecleaner agrees to _____ (clean the next time for half price). If the Client cancels with no warning or less than a twenty-four-hour warning, the Client agrees to _____ (pay half price).

In the event an item is broken by the Housecleaner, the Housecleaner agrees to _____ (replace the item, or pay the deductible on Client's insurance).

The Housecleaner will furnish all supplies and equipment necessary for cleaning and the cost of these is included in the service. Finally it is agreed that this contract can be cancelled by either party upon written notice.

_____ (signed and dated by Client)

_____ (signed and dated by Housecleaner)

# CONCLUSION

Well this is the end — the end of slavery. You have freed yourself from the shackles that formerly bound you. You are free from unrealistic expectations and demands. In addition, you have rallied the troops, deriving help from your children and spouse. You've ceased procrastinating, you've eliminated your clutter and learned a new way to decorate for easier upkeep. You've employed a few tips on curbing the dirt, preventing messes, and finding solutions to frustrating habits. You now know an efficient way to get the cleaning done and have a new appreciation for the value of a few spare minutes. Furthermore, you are better prepared to make purchases that help to lessen your burden at home instead of contributing to it. You even know what to expect if you decide to hire some help.

You've come a long way from slavery to freedom. It took courage to make the necessary changes. Now you and your family can reap the rewards of your determination and hard work. Housework will no longer loom over you. You are in control now. Don't ever relinquish that power. Keep up with your schedule, on top of the clutter. Resist those unnecessary purchases, and keep your family on their toes.

This may be the end for us, but it's a new beginning for you. With your newfound freedom comes opportunities. Now you have more time to pursue all those things that you've been putting off until someday. Someday is *today*. Enjoy it.

# INDEX